Justice
For Joan

Also by Martin Knight

Justice For Joan

The Arundel Murder

Martin Knight

LONDON BOOKS

LONDON BOOKS
39 Lavender Gardens
London SW11 1DJ
www.london-books.co.uk

A catalogue record for this book
is available from the British Library

ISBN 978-0-9568155-7-6

Every effort has been made to locate owners of any copyright material used in
this book. The author apologises for any omissions. Those brought to the
author's attention will be incorporated in future editions.

Printed and bound in Great Britain by
CPI Group (UK) Ltd, Croydon, CR0 4YY

Typeset by Octavo Smith Publishing Services
www.octavosmith.com

This book is dedicated to
Lena Bamber (1922–2013)
and to Tony Brand (1958–2015),
adventurer and friend

ACKNOWLEDGEMENTS

I would like to thank Lena Bamber, who died in 2013. Her dignified and enduring sorrow over her beloved friend's tragic and violent fate demanded that I write this book. She allowed me access and permission to reproduce letters, photographs and other material from her own archives and from the Woodhouse Family Collection in her possession that are used extensively throughout this book.

Appreciation is due to the staff at West Sussex Record Office, who guided me through the police files on the case, and Superintendent Grenville Wilson of Sussex Police, who granted permission for me to view them.

I would also like to thank the following: Jeanne and Paul Kenward for memories of their father and grandfather, ex-Inspector Fred Narborough; several older Arundel residents who wrote to me with their recollections of the case and the various townsfolk I spoke to on my visits; Michael de Larrabeiti for writing *Foxes' Oven*; Ronald Jacks and Linda Wilson for memories of their father and grandfather, private detective Thomas Jacks; and Brian Cathcart for permission to quote from his book *The Case Of Stephen Lawrence*.

Special thanks to Dr Jonathan Oates, the Ealing Borough Archivist and Local History Librarian, who made many helpful suggestions on my manuscript and widened my whole perspective about the case.

Sources and Works Consulted

The following works, archives and collections were consulted in the preparation of this book:

Lena Bamber archive and Woodhouse Family Collection (reproduced throughout); George Orwell, *The Decline Of The English Murder And Other Essays* © Estate of Sonia Brownell Orwell, 1984 (p. 15); *Daily Mail* © DMG Media (pp. 17–18); Keith Simpson, *Forty Years Of Murder* © Keith Simpson, 1978 (pp. 42–3); Fred Narborough, *Murder On My Mind* © Heirs of Fred Narborough, 1959 (pp. 46–7, 59–60, 77, 79, 185, 186, 199); Michael de Larrabeiti, *Foxes' Oven* © Heirs of Michael de Larrabeiti, 2002 (pp. 53–4, 195–6, 202–3); *Daily Express* © Express Newspapers (p. 55); *The Straits Times* © Singapore Press Holdings (p. 81); *Sunday Pictorial* (pp. 90–3); *Yorkshire Post* © Yorkshire Post Newspapers (pp. 100–1); West Sussex Record Office (pp. 114–36 *passim*, p. 199); *Western Morning News* © Local World Ltd (p. 137); *Daily Graphic* (p. 138); *Sunday Chronicle* (p. 138); *Sunday Dispatch* (pp. 143–7, 148–53); *Hull Daily Mail* © Local World Ltd (p. 154); *Yorkshire Evening Press* © Newsquest Media Group (p. 159); *The Times* © News UK (p. 160); *Derby Evening Telegraph* © Sam Jackett (p. 178); Brian Cathcart, *The Case Of Stephen Lawrence* © Brian Cathcart, 2000 (p. 188).

CONTENTS

LIST OF ILLUSTRATIONS

A portrait of Joan Woodhouse taken shortly before her murder *Alamy*

Joan in happier times: sunbathing, 1935; in Folkestone, Kent, 1935, with her aunts, Ida Sheriff and Annie Blades; at University College Library, London, 1947 *Lena Bamber/Woodhouse Family Collection*

The path through Arundel Park showing the slope up to Box Copse where Joan's body was found © *Tony Collis, 2015*

The mock-up picture of Joan and how she would have appeared on the day of her murder issued by the police and published in the press

Thomas Stillwell, the local man who discovered Joan's body and who was later accused of her murder, seen here in his football kit

Foxes' Oven, Offham, West Sussex, today; in 1948 it was the home of the Stillwell family. © *Tony Collis, 2015*

The Black Rabbit, Offham, where Stillwell played darts after discovering Joan's body © *Tony Collis, 2015*

John Woodhouse, Joan's father, had to face the murder of his daughter and a long battle for justice. *Alamy*

Lena Bamber, Joan's friend, with Joan's redoubtable aunts, who visited Arundel regularly after 1948 in their own pursuit of justice *Lena Bamber/Woodhouse Family Collection*

Inspector Fred Narborough, the first Scotland Yard detective to be assigned to the 'Arundel murder' case

Inspector Reg Spooner, the second Yard detective to be assigned to the case, in conversation with Narborough *Alamy*

Thomas Jacks, the private detective from Bridlington, Yorkshire, who was hired by the Woodhouse family to try to succeed where the police had failed *Jacks Family Collection*

Thomas Jacks' business card *Jacks Family Collection*

Spooner at his desk *Alamy*

Spooner and colleague *Alamy*

Stillwell wearing a sling for his 'poisoned finger' *Alamy*

Stillwell on his way to the inquest *Alamy*

Stillwell entering Arundel Town Hall from the rear of the building

Rear entrance to Arundel Town Hall today © *Tony Collis, 2015*

Stuart Bass, the Crown's prosecutor, who bizarrely prefaced his case
against Stillwell by saying, 'Never before in a charge of murder have
you had less evidence.' *Alamy*

Vincent Jackson, the local solicitor who represented Stillwell, arriving at
the hearing at Arundel Town Hall *Alamy*

Witness Mrs Petley, who believed she saw Stillwell in Arundel Park
walking alongside Joan on the day of the murder *Alamy*

Ellen Stillwell, Tom's mother, and Tom's brother Arthur rush to the court

Jurors examine the crime scene around Box Copse

Stillwell's story from the *Sunday Pictorial* of 26 February 1950

Bernard Marmaduke Fitzalan-Howard, 16th Duke of Norfolk and owner
of Arundel Castle *Alamy*

A picture of Stillwell showing a strong facial resemblance to the 16th
Duke *National Portrait Gallery*

Stillwell later in life

A misty view of Arundel Castle from the Black Rabbit pub, Offham, 2015
© *Tony Collis, 2015*

INTRODUCTION

It was on Thursday 12 August 1948 that the name of Joan Woodhouse first entered the British public's consciousness. It would remain embedded there for many years, and even today older citizens, whose formative entertainment was provided by radio and cinema and whose information and titillation came via books and the popular press, can recall the mysterious and desperately sad Arundel murder case when their memories are stirred. In Arundel itself, nestled in rural Sussex, locals have better knowledge than most – personal memories, theories and myths being passed down through generations.

In 1948 Britain was a country recently reinforced in its identity and united by emerging victorious, if ragged, from the Second World War, but the people were increasingly tired of the austerity and hardship visited upon them. Food, clothing and petrol remained rationed. There was little in the way of income to dispose of, and the people gladly absorbed everything they could to divert them from the harshness of day-to-day living. As George Orwell observed, in an essay, 'Decline of the English Murder', published in 1946, two years earlier, murder – or, more accurately, reading about it – was a very British leisure activity. It's a Sunday afternoon in the typical British home. The children are outside playing. Orwell pictured a housewife asleep in her armchair while the husband is settled in his chair, glasses perched on his nose and opening the *News of the World*. The aromas of roast beef and gravy are wafting in from the kitchen. Orwell has him puffing on his pipe as he anticipates settling down to read on about a good, grisly murder. Heaven!

In 1948 the public fascination with murder had recently been fuelled by the exceptionally malevolent exploits of a very British serial killer, Neville Heath, who committed horrendous crimes in Sussex and London.

The London Olympic Games of 1948, just ended, had been a resounding success and Britain had proved a worthy host even if she failed to secure a single gold medal in the all-important athletic events. The games had been dubbed the 'Austerity Games', but hindsight would mark the event as a turning point in Britain's recovery from conflict. Fanny Blankers-Koen, nicknamed the Flying Dutchwoman, was the Mo Farah of the moment after she beat our own shorthand typist Dorothy Manley in the final of the women's 100 metres.

If home-grown sporting prowess did not triumph at the Olympic Games, the event had boosted the national spirit greatly, and sportsmen were excelling almost everywhere else you cared to look. Freddie Mills, a young boxer from Bournemouth whose skills were honed in the unforgiving fairground boxing booths, had just become World Light-Heavyweight Champion, beating the American Gus Lesnevich. There was also immense pride in the England football team, who were still basking in their unexpected, but joyous, 4-0 victory over the mighty and flamboyantly skilful Italy in the spring. The two Stanleys (Matthews and Mortensen) and the two Toms (Finney and Lawton) were an irresistible forward line. Matthews and Mortensen had also featured in the FA Cup Final back in May when their Blackpool side succumbed to Matt Busby's first Manchester United team at Wembley. A momentum was building in English football, which would peak two decades later.

The cinema remained a key source of succour for the masses, just as it had been before and during the war. *Miracle on 34th Street*, starring Maureen O'Hara and child actress Natalie Wood, had charmed the picture-going hordes at Christmas, and when it picked up an Oscar in March for Best Film the public concurred. British picture *The Winslow Boy*, starring Robert Donat, Terence Rattigan's story of a public schoolboy wrongly accused of theft, was a big draw, as was Alfred Hitchcock's adaptation of English writer Patrick Hamilton's play *Rope*, featuring James Stewart and Farley Granger. Hollywood, particularly, still held British audiences firmly in its thrall.

For home entertainment on the wireless *Dick Barton – Special Agent* provided thrills and suspense, the newly launched *Mrs Dale's Diary* some innocent and simple voyeurism into an early 'soap' life and Tommy Handley, with his *It's That Man Again* show, welcome laughter. When Handley died only a few months later national mourning was triggered, and an estimated 10,000 people flocked to the ceremony in Golders Green, London. The wireless united families around a nondescript Bakelite box, with every show and its signature tune providing the rhythms and sound-track of household daily life: *Housewives' Choice*, *Music While You Work*, *Music At Tea-Time*, *Family Favourites*, *Bandstand* and *Sports Report* all marking the time of day.

Newspapers were still devoured religiously and eagerly – nearly four million people read the *Daily Express* alone, and another nine million took one of the *Mirror*, *Herald*, *Mail* or *News Chronicle*. On Sunday, the day of rest, an astonishing eight million souls would be engrossed in the salacious *News Of The World*. Bearing in mind the paper was passed around the household it would be safe to assume that every juicy titbit was enjoyed by more than ten million people, some 20 per cent of the total population. A further twenty million people were reading the rival Sunday papers, including the *Sunday Pictorial* and, with two million sales, a long-forgotten title, *The Empire*.

The newspapers that dropped through letter-boxes that balmy Thursday morning of 12 August, or were purchased with a few brown coppers from newsagents and kiosks up and down the country, were heavy with coverage of the Olympic Games, but, on a sombre note, most carried a portrait photo-graph of Joan Woodhouse, looking elegant, innocent and smiling sweetly, on their front pages. She is smart in a cardigan and necklace, her slightly crooked teeth denoting that, although the photograph is professionally taken, she was no studio model. The portrait conveyed the demeanour of a well-groomed, ordinary librarian with her life in front of her. She was.

The *Daily Mail* splash was typical:

ARUNDEL GIRL IDENTIFIED
Police seeking a man
From Laurence Wilkinson
ARUNDEL, Thursday, 2 a.m.

Police decided early today that the girl found half-dressed and strangled in the bracken of Arundel Castle Park was Joan Woodhouse, 27-year-old London librarian and ex-London University student.

They also have a detailed description of a man they wish to interview – a man who knew Joan well.

Within hours of the body being found on Tuesday police had noted the resemblance between the descriptions in police circulars of Joan Wood-house, missing from a YWCA hostel at Blackheath, SE.

Joan was reported missing by her parents when it was discovered that she had not reached her home in Park Road, Barnsley, Yorkshire, although she had said at the hostel, when she went on holiday on Saturday, July 31, that she was going home.

Police know that she was a modest, demure girl. She wore thick lisle stockings, had bookish tastes even outside her work.

She was not inclined to romantic adventures with men encountered by chance and of whose background she was uncertain.

They believe that when she closed her books and left the quiet atmosphere of the library where she worked, any man with whom she walked would be of tastes similar to her own. Their evening would be spent in some quiet café.

With this picture in mind Detective Superintendent Fred Narborough, of Scotland Yard, and West Sussex detectives are pursuing the task of reconstructing the off-duty life of Joan Woodhouse.

He is considering the possibility that Joan Woodhouse and a man travelled to Littlehampton to spend a day by the seaside then took a bus to Arundel, four miles away.

Hotels and boarding-houses in Littlehampton will be checked to see if anyone answering the description of Joan Woodhouse booked in for a night or for the whole of the Bank Holiday with a man.

Teeth clue

Dr Keith Simpson, Home Office pathologist, after a two-hour autopsy, announced: 'It was a murder.'

His examination had paid special attention to the jaw formation and teeth.

The overlapping of two front teeth tallied with a description of the teeth of Joan Woodhouse.

No formal identification by relatives will now be made. The clothing found in Arundel Park, with fingerprints and certain scientific factors, are believed by police to put the issue beyond question.

The body had been discovered on the Tuesday, 10 August, and had been reported briefly in the press the following morning, but only now, with the identification of the murdered girl, did the story really take off. From the sensationalist press point of view it had it all: a pretty, 'demure' librarian, an ancient and famous castle and bucolic picnic-area, sex and murder, a sleuth from the Yard and a suspect on whose tail the detectives were already attached.

Readers were encouraged to draw their own conclusions, but the newspapers were already directing their readers' thoughts, and Scotland Yard were directing theirs. This attractive librarian was not so demure as perhaps she had led all to believe; she had misled her friends at the Young Women's Christian Association (YWCA) as to her true destination on this bank-holiday Saturday and had a secret assignation planned – a 'dirty weekend' perhaps? Something had gone wrong during a consensual sexual encounter with this gentleman friend as they canoodled in the secluded grounds of Arundel Park under the aristocratic shadow of the castle; this 'friend' had strangled her and scarpered. Those dogged detectives from the Yard would soon catch the blighter, and he'd be brought to justice, tried at the Old Bailey and eventually hanged by the neck by Pierrepoint. (Mr Albert Pierrepoint was Britain's unofficial official hangman for many years, and some estimate that he personally lynched up to six hundred people.)

It was a familiar chain of events, and the public looked forward to them unfolding, along with all the gory and salacious detail that would undoubtedly accompany the process in their newspaper columns as they were encouraged literally to read between the lines.

In the *Evening Argus* in Sussex an explicit and disturbing picture had appeared on 11 August of the body in the undergrowth before the corpse's identification. It shows the dead victim in a state of undress, legs apart. It is a shocking image and one that would never be permitted publication in a newspaper today. It must have been taken by or with the knowledge and permission of a police officer, and as such is a gross compromise of a crime scene and an unforgivable breach of privacy and abuse of a family's sensibilities. (And we thought that the *News Of The World* in the early years of the twenty-first century overstepped the mark.) One can only hope that Joan's family and friends did not have to see this photograph, although it is unlikely they were spared.

However, this was to prove to be no open-and-shut case, and the *Mail* article was just the beginning of a lengthy, eventful journey that would impact negatively on a number of lives and careers besides that of the deceased. The aftermath would resonate down the decades.

The man Scotland Yard had in their sights and who is referred to in those initial press reports was Edward 'Ted' Roberts, also a respectable librarian, who would soon demonstrate he was not with Joan on that bank holiday and had not seen her for some time and could prove it. The Yard, however, was not to be deterred – their theory still held. If Ted Roberts was 'alibied' it must have been another man, yet to be identified, whom she had arranged the alfresco tryst with. The trawl of boarding-houses mentioned in the newspapers was fruitless – Joan had not booked in anywhere for the night or the weekend either alone or with a man. Her travel case, lightly packed, was found in the left-luggage office at Worthing Station. She had been seen in Arundel, according to some early eye witnesses, on Saturday 31 July, the pathologist's estimated day of her death – alone.

Over the ensuing few months elite Scotland Yard detectives attempted to crack the case and failed. Joan's family were distraught and dissatisfied and hired a private detective to investigate, and he soon fingered the man he believed to be the murderer. Scotland Yard investigated again, drafting in a new detective, but again decided not to prefer charges and closed the inquiry for the second time. They said the evidence against the man was circumstantial and there was no case to warrant a charge. Joan's formidable family vigorously disagreed and launched a private prosecution for murder, the first and only one in England during the twentieth century, but ultimately failed to secure a committal to trial for their suspect.

The Woodhouses' struggle against the police, the legal system and ultimately the Establishment was echoed half a century later when the family of the black teenager Stephen Lawrence felt compelled to launch their own private prosecution to secure justice for their son, who had been murdered in a racially motivated attack. They encountered police incompetence, obstinacy and dishonesty and an Establishment cabal pulling together to block transparency and justice. This book will argue that the family of Joan Woodhouse came up against a similar response.

More than sixty-five years later the Joan Woodhouse murder is officially unsolved and intermittently appears in true-crime magazines and books and occasionally on television. It has become a staple of the twentieth-century murder canon, Joan's name jostling for grisly space with the likes of Neville Heath, Bywaters and Thompson, the Brides In The Bath killer, Haigh (The Acid Bath Murderer), Christopher Craig and Derek Bentley *et al.*, her story re-created for the benefit of murder aficionados from newspaper cuttings, detectives' memoirs and the like. Errors are recycled, assumptions taken as read, opinions paraded as fact. They do little justice to the real story, to Joan Woodhouse and her family, to the key suspect and to the detectives.

I first came across the case back in the 1980s when reading Home Office pathologist Professor Keith Simpson's surprise smash-hit true-crime memoirs *Forty Years Of Murder*. The excerpt on the Arundel murder always stuck in my mind. At the time I worked in a library, like Joan; Woodhouse was a name in my extended family; my parents had taken my siblings and I on trips to Arundel Castle. But unlike most of the other murders in this informative, gripping but macabre book it was unsolved. Professor Simpson is clear that he harboured some scepticism about the police investigation and its conclusions.

In 2010, while internet browsing, I tapped Joan's name in and refreshed my memory about the case. One small item came up from a Littlehampton newspaper on the occasion of the sixtieth anniversary of the murder that mentioned a friend of Joan's called Lena Bamber. She was thanking the readers of this local paper for remembering Joan on this sad anniversary. I looked Lena up and found that she was alive and living in the Midlands. I dialled her number. I'm not sure why.

This lady, then approaching ninety years of age, was overjoyed to hear from me but, strangely, not at all surprised or shocked. She was a devoutly religious woman and said she had been praying the previous night that she should not leave this earth without having secured justice or, at least, explanations for Joan's death and the failed investigation. I said that I could not achieve the former, but if I wrote a book about the case we might help provide some of the latter. She behaved as if she were expecting my telephone call as a matter of routine, such was her faith in her God.

On a subsequent visit to Lena's house in Heanor, Derbyshire, she presented me with a battered leather briefcase with the initials JTW embossed in faded gold plate on the front. It was a remnant of the era when all briefcases and suitcases were a muddy brown. This belonged to Joan's father, John Thomas Woodhouse, and he had passed his sad dossier on to Lena.

On flicking the creaking catches open I was transported back to the middle of the previous century and the very personal and real tragedy of a young woman and her distraught family. It contained reams of letters, press cuttings and photographs charting the whole history of Joan's life, the case and the family's fight for justice – a legal David-and-Goliath battle that I soon saw featured some of the best-known Establishment names of the era. I was engrossed and saddened simultaneously, feeling Mr Woodhouse's tragedy, pain and frustration seeping out of the yellowed, fraying contents of the case. As I travelled home down the motorway that night, my head spinning and the beam of my headlights swallowing road markings like Pac-Man, I felt strongly that a baton had been passed to me and that there was not much I could do about it.

Lena was a remarkable lady. She had been a headmistress at Marlpool Infant School in Heanor for many years and was obviously much loved and respected in her community. Former pupils corresponded with her and visited on a regular basis, despite her having been retired for forty years or more. She had never married and by now was not moving too much from her chair in a room surrounded by antiques she had lovingly collected over the years. Her brain remained sharp, and I could see she was troubled. Her life was ebbing away, and she knew it, and although she had fulfilled her promise to Joan's father and family to continue the fight for Joan after their deaths she had not succeeded (in her eyes) in securing justice for her dear friend. She had wanted the murderer to be brought to book; she had wanted Joan's name to be cleared. Her friend had been a pure, God-fearing woman, and the world should know that. She considered the sexual innuendo that surrounded Joan an abomination of the gravest kind.

By 2013 Lena's health had deteriorated considerably, and she entered hospital and eventually died. I was able to tell her that this book would be published, and she did read and comment on an early draft. Her relatives told me at the funeral that she drew great comfort from that.

In *Justice For Joan* I have endeavoured to present fuller facts and background information, some of which have never been placed in the public domain before, even in court. I hope I have presented it as dispassionately as possible. The question is raised as to whether there were other forces at work beyond the immediate question of a man's guilt or innocence. Was a terrible miscarriage of justice narrowly avoided, or did a murderer walk free and live the long life Joan could not? At the end of the book I hope the reader is, at least, far better informed about this troubling case and will be better placed to draw their personal conclusion as to what really happened to Joan Woodhouse on that boiling hot Saturday afternoon in July 1948.

1
RULE OF LIFE

Joan Mary Woodhouse was born in Barnsley, Yorkshire on 17 July 1921 to John Thomas Woodhouse and his wife Nellie, née Wilkinson. Joan's mother came from a large Barnsley working-class family, her father supporting them all as a glovemaker. Among Nellie's older sisters were Ida and Annie, who would find their later lives overshadowed and dominated by the dreadful fate of their young sibling and her tragic family.

Joan was an only child to the church-going, God-fearing John and Nellie and enjoyed their undivided attention and love. John was a youth worker – a job that allowed him to put something back into society, chiming with his religious beliefs – and Nellie was a teacher at the local grammar school, coaching the children in needlework and weaving. John Thomas Woodhouse came from mining stock, and John himself had once worked down the pit. John's father, William Maskery Woodhouse, had been a coalminer, but on his marriage certificate John described his father as a professional musician.

In 1943 this happy family unit was shattered when Nellie developed cancer and subsequently died at the tragically young age of 46. Joan's aunties, Ida Sheriff and Annie Blades, known as Nida and Nan respectively to the young girl, did everything they could to fill their dead sister's shoes. They lived in the seaside town of Bridlington, also in Yorkshire but some eighty miles away, and Joan was a regular visitor before and after her mother's death. The relationship between the two aunts and their niece was a close and loving one and intensified following the premature death of Nellie.

Both aunts were widows. Annie had married Adam Blades, a lance corporal in the Yorkshire and Lancashire Regiment in 1916, conscious, almost certainly, that time might be short as a world war was raging and taking a terrible toll in human life. It did. Adam was killed in action in

Belgium just over a year later at only twenty-eight years of age. He left £193 to his brother-in-law Arthur Sheriff, Ida's husband and the son of a shrimp-dealer from Hull, presumably so he could provide for his wife with it – after all, those were times when many men considered that women were not able to manage such things as significant sums of money.

Tragically, Arthur himself died at the even younger age of twenty-six in the flu pandemic of 1918 that claimed more lives globally than the war. The two sisters, now yoked together by grief and tragedy, closed ranks and became inseparable. When Joan was born only three years later to their next-closest-in-age sister, Nellie, she came to represent the child they both knew now they would never have.

In a photograph album of Joan's short life, poignantly and lovingly compiled by her aunts after her death, it is clear that the family enjoyed an above-average standard of living. A nanny is evident in baby pictures as are a number of foreign holidays as the years pass. This is some decades before the era of cheap flights and annual sojourns to the Mediterranean. Joan also developed religious leanings early in life, no doubt inspired and encouraged by her parents, but the young girl's commitment was soon to grow beyond even her parents' faith. She became very active in the Anglican Church, embracing the religion more fully as each year passed. As an adult she attended confession and went to mass each morning on waking.

She performed well academically at Barnsley Girls' High School and won a place at the University of London in Bloomsbury, where she studied and qualified in librarianship. As part of her further education she followed her mother's profession and took on short-term teaching assignments at local schools in the West Riding of Yorkshire.

During the Second World War her educational path was interrupted when she was called up for service. She attended a training school in Sheffield, where she studied draughtsmanship. Women were being encouraged to learn 'men's jobs' while the men were away fighting. Here she met a Derbyshire girl called Lena Bamber, and they struck up a friendship that endured for the rest of Joan's life. In 2010 Lena recalled their first meeting:

Joan made a big impression on me immediately. She was sparkling and full of life. She was just so happy. That first lunchtime at Sheffield she had an orange, and when she peeled it she broke it into segments and passed it around until she was left with just one piece, if that. Remember, we were all complete strangers.

After the war, Joan landed a job with the National Library in London after gaining her degree. At this time it was part of the British Museum and housed the country's literary collection. She was overjoyed and her family immensely proud. Joan began working in the department that distributed rare books and was earning a salary of £322 per annum, which equates to some £20,000 today.

Joan took a room in a flat in London's Baker Street, fictional home to detective Sherlock Holmes and around the corner from the tourist destinations of Madame Tussauds, Regent's Park and London Zoo. She relished her new life in the bustling, cosmopolitan metropolis – such a contrast to the archetypal northern working-class town of Barnsley. She adored her work and made many new friends in librarianship circles and soon had a busy social diary. Joan loved attending the Proms and more than once queued all night to ensure she obtained tickets to attend the annual festival at the Royal Albert Hall. She loved books, films and classical music. Her deep faith did not appear at odds with her lust for life. She wrote in one friend's autograph book: 'Be inspired with the belief of a high and noble calling.'

Fathers Morrell and Seebold from Joan's Barnsley church were much impressed at Joan's thirst for religious enlightenment, the former commenting after her death that she had travelled further spiritually in her twenty-seven years than most did in a lifetime and the latter making her godmother to two of his own children. She had joined the Third Order, attached to the Society Of The Sacred Mission, a group within the Anglican Church. The Third Order was made up of men and women who believed that God was calling them to live out their faith in the world, in their homes and in their normal daily lives. Those who belonged to the order lived under a Rule of Life that they were expected to sign up to once they believed they could be governed by it. The Society Of The Sacred Mission provided a spiritual director to guide members and arranged meetings in which they could meet, discuss and develop their calling.

On 31 October 1946 Joan committed to and signed her own personal Rule of Life. It reads as follows:

I will offer my day's work to God on waking.

Pray for at least five minutes in the morning and at least twenty minutes at night.

Say the Company Office and the Society prayer each midday.

Make an examination of the day's work each evening.

Be at Mass on Sundays and Holy Days and make my communion at least once each week.

Make one-quarter-of-an-hour meditations each week and make an annual retreat.

Do one hour spiritual reading each week.

Read a chapter of the Bible each day.

Make my confession monthly.

Seek out opportunities for helping others.

Give at least one quarter of my personal money as alms.

Fast on Fridays and other fast days.

Keep an account of my expenditure.

Practice [sic] interior mortification.

Be in bed by 11 p.m.

It was a stiff undertaking even by the stricter religious standards of the day. One imagines that a modern-day Christian, or even a man or woman of the Church, would find it onerous to abide by each and every one of these rules.

One example of Joan's practical interpretation of Rule 10, for example, was when a Jamaican fellow-student at the University of London named Monica told her of her difficulty in securing accommodation in the capital. Joan was appalled at how landlords and landladies were slamming doors in her face and how one house-owner had even spat at her. This was a time when landlords routinely posted notices on their doors and in windows declaring: 'No blacks. No Irish. No dogs.' Newspapers routinely referred to the 'colour problem' and the 'colour bar', and casual racism was the norm not the exception.

Joan went out with Monica the next day, traipsing the London streets on the hunt for a room, standing literally shoulder to shoulder with the frightened Jamaican until the girl was finally granted a place to live. Monica, who later married a surgeon and returned to work in a leading hospital in

Kingston, Jamaica, never forgot Joan's kindness and determination.

In December 1947 Joan's father remarried, to a lady named Hilda Cowdell, who was twenty-four years his junior and only slightly older than Joan herself. Four years had passed since Joan had lost her mother and John his wife. How Joan took this potentially unsettling development is undocumented, but she was a witness at the marriage ceremony, which was conducted by Father John Seebold and, in later letters to her aunt, she states that Hilda was always kind and generous to her. Around this time Joan's aunts became aware that she had formed a close friendship with another librarian, a man named Ted Roberts.

If gaining a stepmother of almost her own age did not upset Joan's equilibrium too greatly, the relationship with Ted Roberts did. Ted was a fellow librarian, also at the beginning of his career. The relationship was eventually called off and caused Joan much anguish. Her friends believed they were planning to become engaged, but there had been some difficulty over Joan's deep religious convictions. Ted is thought to have ended the romance. Joan became distraught, and during the early months of 1948 sunk into a severe depression. She retreated to Bridlington, to her aunts, and opened her heart to them. They were worried and could see their beloved niece was deeply troubled. She confessed that she had half-heartedly attempted suicide and had even written a suicide note before taking aspirin. When she awoke with no obvious damage she was appalled, as in her religious teachings this was considered the ultimate sin. This sad incident has been dated as taking place on 28 March 1948.

Ida and Annie advised her to leave the Baker Street flat where she was now living on her own. They wanted her to be among people at all times, and Joan could see the sense in this. She made plans to live at a hostel among young, vibrant Christian professionals such as herself. While visiting her father in Barnsley she went to see Father Seebold and confessed her sin – namely the attempt at and consideration of suicide – and he gave her absolution. She returned to London more settled, but her two aunts remained deeply troubled.

Shortly before the depression had enveloped Joan, Lena Bamber can recall visiting the seaside resort of Scarborough with her. One memory is etched deeply in her mind, and even in 2010, more than sixty years later, Lena could conjure up her friend in one brief moment on that holiday. She is dancing and fooling around in the sea, kicking her legs and splashing, her arms flung wide and loudly proclaiming Shakespeare, 'this sceptred isle . . . set in a silver sea . . . this earth, this realm, this England'.

For Lena it is a treasured memory. It encapsulates everything about her best and dearest girlfriend. Her love of life, her energy, her sense of the time and the place and her sense of fun. It is *the* memory that Lena uses to blot the rest out.

2

'ARE YOU OK?
IF NOT, COME HOME.
AUNTIE IS WORRIED'

Taking Nida and Nan's advice, Joan moved into the Young Women's Christian Association (YWCA) hostel at 29 Bennett Park, Blackheath, south-east London. Blackheath is often referred to as a village, but then, as now, it was one of the more salubrious London areas, boasting open green spaces and panoramic views of the surrounding landscape. Bennett Park itself was a road of large Victorian houses, some divided into flats, that began almost opposite Blackheath railway station.

At the YWCA Joan met another resident, Nicole Ashby, and they quickly struck up a sadly short, but strong, friendship. Joan became popular among the staff and other residents. When questioned by the police in the days after the murder none of them reported having detected any serious depression in her, although some were aware of the failed relationship with Ted Roberts.

In 2015 Nicole emailed me. Even after almost seventy years it was clear that having been embroiled in a murder case remained traumatic for her. She reiterated Joan's deep religious conviction, recalling that she attended Donald Soper's sermons in Kingsway Hall, London, every Sunday morning. Soper was a Methodist preacher and pacifist whose rallies attracted people from near and far. His mantra that 'love and trust and sacrifice are the weapons which are perfectly effectual to achieve all that men have tried – and failed – to secure by terror and the sword' resonated with Joan. Nicole attended, too, and remembers Soper's charismatic oratory.

In the hot summer of 1948 London was fizzing with excitement over the Olympic Games, the first since 1936 because of the Second World War. That momentous event dictated that Germany and Japan would not be competing in this tournament. They were firmly sat on the international naughty step. Two and half million tickets were sold, and roads as well as train and bus stations were packed all across the capital. Ration books were still required to obtain certain foods, and the scarring of the landscape after the aerial bombardment was everywhere, but the games were a beacon of hope. Proof, if it were needed, that London was alive and well and functioning.

In this year Aneurin Bevan launched the National Health Service, a development that would have heartened Joan as it pledged to provide free medicine and care to everyone regardless of their background and means. On the international stage, the State of Israel had been formed and Mahatma Ghandi was assassinated. The Second World War may have ended, but the peace was only slightly less eventful.

Joan may well have gone to see the film *Oliver Twist* at the cinema. Starring Alec Guinness as Fagin and John Howard Davies as young Oliver, it was playing to packed audiences throughout June and July. Shot in grainy black and white, with its gritty and atmospheric depiction of poverty, deprivation and low-life existence in Victorian London, it was a far cry from the happy-go-lucky, cheeky-cockney-caper musical that was filmed thirty years later with Ron Moody and Jack Wild.

Joan could not have avoided hearing 'Nature Boy' by Nat King Cole, one of the most popular tunes of that hot, balmy summer. Another, 'The Woody Woodpecker Song', sung by American film star and comedian Danny Kaye (who had recently captivated the country at the London Palladium), would have especially resonated with Joan, as her colleagues and fellow residents at the YWCA had taken to calling her Woody.

Her aunts were encouraged by letters received from their niece during June and July of 1948, in which she told them about Nicole, the hostel and various parties, dinners and social occasions she had attended. On Saturday 17 July 1948 Joan celebrated her twenty-seventh birthday. Nida, Annie and John Woodhouse all cautiously felt that the worst for Joan had passed and their delicate, fragile Barnsley lass down in London, in the Big Smoke, who had been through so much in the last few years, was going to be fine.

However, in a letter dated 28 July, Joan did make statements indicative of depression, which triggered panic again in her two aunts. One passage read: 'I wonder what sort of future I have. No interests, no friends, no job. I can't go on like this forever.' She must have written this during a particularly black episode because she had many friends and was highly thought of at her work, and she must have known this.

Temperatures rose along with public excitement on that bank-holiday weekend in 1948. The games had opened on Thursday 29 July, but the crowds were expected to peak on the Saturday. Joan decided to get out of London and head up north to visit her father and aunts for the whole bank-holiday weekend, leaving on Saturday morning and returning Monday night. At least, that is what she intimated to her family and friends. It had been widely reported that getting around London on its rail, bus and tram infrastructure was going to be a nightmare and, like many Londoners, Joan probably felt it would be a good idea to be elsewhere other than the capital for the weekend.

Nicole Ashby, her friend at the hostel, said Joan ate breakfast early on the Saturday morning and seemed happy and in high spirits. She was dressed gaily in a blue Paisley dress with yellow and pink stripes, blue lace gloves and blue sandals. Nicole remembered in 2015 that Joan had dyed the sandals from beige at the hostel. As well as her suitcase she carried her overcoat and mackintosh. Nicole was sure she had said she was heading up to the family home in Barnsley. She added that Joan had invited her that morning to travel up to Charing Cross with her for the ride. She sees this as negating theories that Joan was planning a clandestine meeting with anyone.

The excessive outerwear Joan took with her on that extremely hot day has suggested to some observers of the case that she was not quite with it on Saturday morning, that her mind was preoccupied with something. It was already baking, and that Saturday would end up being one of the hottest days of the twentieth century, with temperatures hitting the upper nineties Fahrenheit. Someone in their right frame of mind would not have dreamed of carrying an overcoat, they have pointed out. However, others have commented that Joan was wise to the vagaries of the English weather – especially in the north – and elected to take outerwear for all eventualities.

Before she and Nicole parted, at about 8.30 a.m., Joan mentioned she was catching the 10.10 a.m. train from King's Cross and chalked her name up on the board for attending dinner at the YWCA the following Tuesday evening. Nicole Ashby would be the last known person who actually *knew* Joan to see her alive, so far as is known.

She did not catch that 10.10 a.m. train from King's Cross. Instead, and this is one of the most inexplicable facets of the whole case, she ended up at midday at Worthing Station on the south coast of England, where she deposited her travelling case in the left-luggage office and was issued with a ticket. She did not deposit her overcoat or mackintosh. The journey from Victoria Station to Worthing would have taken about seventy-five minutes. Getting from Blackheath to Victoria is a twenty-minute journey. One might assume two lots of fifteen minutes waiting time. This equates to about two hours fifteen minutes travelling time, meaning that if Worthing was where Joan had decided to go first she should have arrived between 10.45 and 11.00 a.m. at the latest. An hour, at least, before she actually did.

Arundel is around eleven miles from Worthing, and Joan, after depositing her case at Worthing station, took a train or a bus there. As she was already on the rail network it is more likely she travelled the single stop on the train. Again, there is a considerable gap between when she should or could have been seen in Arundel and when she first was. Theoretically she should have alighted in Arundel between 12.30 and 1 p.m., at the latest, but she is first sighted in a shop buying a bottle of Lembar – a lemon-and-barley-water soft drink – at around 2 p.m. Giving support to this first alleged sighting is a second from a Miss Gwendoline Dibley, who came forward to say she saw a lady looking like Joan walking down Mill Road towards Arundel Park at about 2.15 p.m.

Joan did not return that afternoon or evening to collect her case from Worthing station. Nor did she appear at her father's house in Barnsley or at her aunts' flat in Bridlington. Most worryingly she did not arrive back at the hostel on Tuesday and was noticeably absent at dinner.

On the Wednesday morning the head librarian at the National Library, Joan's line manager, rang the YWCA to see if she was unwell, as she had not come to work or phoned in sick. Alarm bells began to ring ominously. At the same time, up in Barnsley and Bridlington, Joan's family began to sense something was seriously amiss. John Woodhouse sent a telegram to the hostel on Wednesday 4 August, which arrived on Thursday. It read: 'Are you OK? If not come home. Auntie is worried.'

The fact that Joan was not at the family home alarmed Jessie Maddocks, the warden hostel, when she absorbed the implications of the telegram. She immediately wired back to Mr Woodhouse and then walked straight into Lee Road Police Station on Lee High Road, about a mile from the hostel, and reported Joan as a missing person. Later that night she wrote a longer letter to Mr Woodhouse expressing her rising alarm. As soon as the telegram from the hostel with its worrying reply was delivered to 237 Park Road in Barnsley, John Woodhouse rang his sisters-in-law and between them they decided that John and Ida would travel down to London and Annie would remain at home in case Joan turned up there. For all their sakes they tried to suppress their building panic.

On Saturday morning Joan's father and aunt arrived at the hostel and spoke to Nicole and Jessie and heard about Joan's departure a week before. Now they knew in their bones that some disaster had befallen Joan and, with hearts in mouths, they, too, visited the police station. Predictably, the police did not share John and Ida's acute concern and attempted to dampen down their worst fears. Joan was twenty-seven years old, they said, not twelve. She would turn up in good time. Most do. Try not to worry.

Protecting Joan's privacy, John and Ida did not immediately inform the police of her recent depression, although Joan's aunt was back in the station the following day determined to galvanise them into doing something, telling them everything she knew about her niece. This time, knowing there was a real risk that Joan may have harmed herself, she was listed officially as a missing person. Lee Road Police Station duly filed the following report for circulation to all police stations:

PERSONS MISSING

Joan Woodhouse. YWCA 29 Bennetts Park, SE3 (home address 237 Park Road, Barnsley, Yorkshire). Aged twenty-seven, librarian, five feet, slim build, complexion sallow, eyes blue, straight nose, oval face, two front teeth overlap, mole right side of upper lip. Reserved. Wearing fawn tweed coat, multi-coloured frock, cherry-coloured woollen cardigan, string of pearls, two diamond rings right hand, carried brown handbag and blue weekend case. Had quarrelled with her fiancé. Intended visiting her home but failed to arrive. Recently recovered from a nervous breakdown. It is feared she may commit suicide.

It was now Sunday 8 August 1948. Distraught, distressed and terrified of what the coming days would bring, John Woodhouse and Ida Sheriff boarded a train home from King's Cross station. It was a long, sombre journey from London back to Yorkshire, with a sense of heavy foreboding almost tangible like an unwanted passenger settling between them.

3
BOX COPSE

The 'Domesday Book' records that Arundel was a busy market town of a few hundred residents by 1086. The castle had been built some twenty years earlier by the Norman Lord Roger de Montgomery, following William the Conqueror's victory at the Battle of Hastings. In 1243 the castle came to be owned by the Fitzalan family and, at the end of the 16th century, it was acquired, along with all the land, by the Duke of Norfolk. Strange, perhaps, that the Duke of Norfolk should own large swathes of Sussex, but the aristocracy moved in such ways.

In 1948 the town was home to some 1,000 dwellings and 3,000 people and was already a well-established tourist attraction. The advent of the motor car had brought in the Sunday drivers, who explored the castle and its grounds and took refreshment in the rustic tea rooms. Surrounded by farmland and open country, the inhabitants were mainly rural folk or the comfortably retired, swelled considerably in the summer by visitors keen to take in the castle, its grounds and the river as well as Arundel Cathedral, the Georgian architecture and the 'olde worlde' welcome of the town itself. Although only fifty miles from London and eighteen from Brighton, the town was bucolic and largely crime-free. The local people, in 1948 at least, were often referred to as 'mullets' after the sea fish that often made it up the River Arun that runs along the eastern side of the town.

The incumbent Duke of Norfolk in 1948 was Bernard Marmaduke Fitzalan-Howard, known locally as Duke Bernard. He was a popular man with the people of Arundel, being a big local employer and champion of the town. Many remember him as having the common touch and, even now, older residents refer to him as the Duke *for* Arundel. His wife Lavinia was also enormously popular in the town and is remembered today with great affection.

Duke Bernard was born in 1908 and lived a full and varied life until his death in 1975. He served in the Second World War and was wounded in action. He was an enthusiastic owner of racehorses and an avid cricket fan (although an average player) and, incongruously became the manager of the English cricket team in Australia in 1962–3. He is arguably best remembered for his role as Hereditary Earl Marshal, a role in which he was obliged to organise the marriage ceremony of George VI and Elizabeth Bowes-Lyon, the Queen Mother. He also oversaw the coronation of Elizabeth II and the investiture of Prince Charles as the Prince of Wales at Caernarvon Castle. In 1965 Duke Bernard was famously tasked with staging Winston Churchill's funeral, which was to be a huge global television event. His most famous touch was to arrange for construction cranes on the docks of the Thames to lower their jibs in respect as Churchill's coffin passed them on a boat.

Some time just after 5 p.m. on Tuesday 10 August 1948 Sergeant Bristow stood behind the desk of Arundel Police Station when a man hurriedly parked a bicycle against an outside wall and burst through the door. He was in an excitable state and attempting to catch his breath.

'I've found a body in the park. At Box Copse,' he spluttered. 'It's a girl.'

Bristow called out to his colleague PC Wood, and they fetched their motorbikes from behind the station building on the Causeway and rode down Mill Road, turning left into the park gates at Swanbourne Lake and following the path around the perimeter of the lake until Box Copse, a small hilltop of beech trees and box bushes about fifteen feet high, loomed up beside them.

Following them and pedalling furiously on the pushbike was the man who had reported finding the body. He was a local labourer, house-painter and odd-job man in his middle twenties named Thomas Philip George Stillwell. The officers had had no reason to doubt him. The two policemen paused at the foot of Box Copse as they waited for Stillwell to catch up and take them to the exact spot where he had discovered the corpse.

The three men climbed the hill, and Stillwell pointed over to the body as it came into view. There had been no attempt at concealment. Straight away the policemen could see it was a female. The dead girl was lying on her back, face upwards, stretched out across the slope, with her legs slightly apart. She was clothed only in pink camiknickers, bra, elastic suspender belt attached to stockings and sandals. Shocked, they surveyed the scene, and as their eyes travelled further up the slope they saw a pile of women's clothes – wet but folded neatly. As they walked towards them and passed the girl's head they realised for the first time that the face was extremely decomposed and the features unrecognisable.

Sergeant Bristow felt uneasy and queasy. His instinct told him this was no death from natural causes. Something was wrong, very wrong. He needed to protect what could be a murder scene right away and alert his superior, Detective Inspector William Dean (nicknamed 'Dixie' after the Everton and England high-scoring centre-forward) from Littlehampton Criminal Investigation Department (CID). He left PC Wood at the scene, dismissed Thomas Stillwell and roared away on his motorbike. PC Wood stood guard at Box Copse while Stillwell set off, first to his home – a farm labourer's cottage called Foxes' Oven in nearby Offham, owned by the Duke of Norfolk, master of the Arundel estate – for tea and then later that evening to the Black Rabbit pub on Mill Road where he played darts with other locals, as he often did.

Detective Inspector Dean, grasping the situation immediately, was not taking any chances and sought assistance from Scotland Yard. The Yard had a famous and sophisticated mobile murder squad that was often called in by regional police forces across the country to assist in less-than-straightforward cases of suspected murder. It was a tried-and-tested practice. The following morning, Wednesday 11 August, Metropolitan Police Deputy Commander William Rawlings dispatched Inspector Frederick Narborough with colleague Detective Sergeant Pattison to assist the local force. At the same time the country's leading police pathologist, Dr Keith Simpson, was travelling to the scene by rail to meet them. It was a heavyweight team indeed.

Fred Narborough was born in 1903 in the tiny village of Wiggenhall St Mary Magdalen in fenland Norfolk, a rural community of just a few hundred souls. The village was two miles from the nearest railway station and seven miles from King's Lynn, the closest town. Fred was raised in the fields, farms and woods of the surrounding countryside but displayed an academic flair and passed through the village school to Thetford Grammar and then Norwich Grammar School.

At the young age of seventeen Fred and his brother were set up on a farm by their father, John Edward, who had prospered himself and, by this time, owned and farmed 1,300 acres. However, financial disaster soon struck when the agricultural slump of the 1920s bankrupted John, and Fred was forced to become an employee, as opposed to employer, on another farm. A career in agriculture now seemed a sour choice, and the young man looked for a way out.

He eventually found this by joining the police, first at Ipswich, but soon afterwards in London. Scotland Yard had been impressed by character references Fred was somehow able to supply from the Lord Mayor of Norwich, the headmaster of Norwich Grammar School and the Chief Constable of Suffolk. In 1924 PC Fred Narborough reported for duty at Hackney Police Station. Only a year later he was in plain clothes fulfilling his ambition to become a detective. He was in the Metropolitan Police fast lane.

By 1945 Narborough had progressed through the Flying Squad to the Murder Squad, and had built a formidable reputation as a tough, determined policeman along the way. He was the man who first put Billy Hill – the self-proclaimed King Of The Underworld – behind bars. *Boss Of Britain's Underworld*, Hill's ghost-written autobiography, propelled him towards becoming the first British celebrity gangster, feared in his pomp and lauded in his retirement in Brighton by the likes of the Kray Twins and assorted showbusiness types. Fred Narborough has also been credited with smashing the racecourse razor gangs that formed a backdrop plot to Graham Greene's iconic, atmospheric novel *Brighton Rock* and the subsequent film starring Richard Attenborough as the dangerous young gangster Pinky.

In the same way Hill evolved into a celebrity gangster, Narborough's career coincided with an era of celebrity policemen and, on a smaller scale, he became famous himself. From the 1930s to the 1960s a group of detectives were household names: Greeno, Fabian, Capstick, Cherrill, Wickstead, Spooner, Read, Slipper and more. They were heroes in trilby hats and dark overcoats, latched on to enthusiastically by an entertainment-hungry public.

Narborough was certainly one of this illustrious group of detectives, and in the top echelon known as the Big Five, the others being Bob Fabian, Bob Stevens, Guy Mahon and Jack Capstick, although, besides the Joan Wood-house case, few of his murder investigations were as famous as the ones investigated by some of his contemporaries. Their cases filled the news-paper columns and became the subjects of films, magazine features and TV programmes. Some of these policemen, including Narborough, embraced the medium of television enthusiastically in retirement, presenting crime programmes of their own.

All this was in the future, though. As Fred Narborough surveyed the murder scene that morning in Arundel he was at the top of his game. A fit, thick-set, pugnacious-looking forty-five-year-old, he did not yet know that this case would be the one that would end his Yard ascent and haunt and trouble him for the rest of his life.

Only a couple of weeks before arriving in Arundel Fred Narborough had made the national newspapers on a non-police matter. He had complained to Aage Thaarup, milliners to the Queen, that they should halve the salary of his seventeen-year-old daughter Jeanne, who was earning £21 a week, while he, a member of Scotland Yard's venerable murder squad, earned less than that. He was making a point about society's values. Thaarup agreed, and Jeanne is quoted diplomatically saying, 'I do not agree with Daddy, but I saw his point that so much money is not good for me. Perhaps he is right, but I will earn much more money when I'm older.'

Jeanne's son, Paul Kenward, Fred's grandson, remembers his grandfather as a tough, sometimes abrasive man. He said that when he was a youth and Fred was a fit pensioner they sometimes clashed. It was a textbook case of the younger generation and the older generation failing to understand and respect each other. This friction culminated one family Christmas with the man and youth exchanging punches after drinks in the local pub before Christmas dinner. Paul retains the image of Fred outside the house shovelling snow and refusing to come in for dinner until an apology was offered.

Dr Cedric Keith Simpson, the son of a GP, was born in Brighton, Sussex, in 1907. Following hard in the footsteps of the revered forensic Yard pathologist Sir Bernard Spilsbury he raised the public awareness of the science of pathology as a key witness in nearly all the famous murder cases of his era. Keith Simpson (he dropped the Cedric) had performed his first post-mortem in 1934, but his profile rose dramatically after 1947 following the death of his colleague Spilsbury. Simpson's casebook is practically an encyclopaedia of twentieth-century murders and murderers. The pathologist's first sensational case was the slaying of Joan Pearl Wolfe by a Canadian soldier, August Sangret, on Hankley Common in Surrey in 1942, in a crime that became known as the Wigwam Murder. Greeno of the Yard led the police investigation into a case that captivated the public through its revelations about illicit sex, unwanted pregnancies and extreme violence. Dr Simpson was able to tell police that the murder had been committed with a knife that had a blade shaped like a parrot's beak. The discovery of such a knife was crucial in incriminating Sangret, and he was hanged at Wandsworth Prison the following year – Albert Pierrepoint, naturally, doing the honours.

In 1949, after Joan's murder, Dr Simpson famously found and identified the gallstones of a Mrs Durand-Deacon in the slurry at John George Haigh's lock-up in Crawley, Sussex, where the killer almost got away with the 'perfect' murders after destroying the bodies of his six victims in a bath of acid. Haigh was convicted only of the murder of Mrs Durand-Deacon, although he claimed he had actually killed nine. His motive was greed, and after murdering and dissolving the bodies in sulphuric acid he wasted no time in forging documents belonging to his victims and systematically plundering their assets. Mrs Durand-Deacon was a rich widow who had had the misfortune of being a resident at the Onslow Court Hotel in London where Haigh had been living as he frittered away his ill-gotten gains. Sir Hartley Shawcross led for the prosecution once Haigh reached Lewes Assizes, and Justice Travers Humphrey sentenced him to death – both men featuring later in this story.

Later still, Dr Simpson was on the John Reginald Christie case, committed to screen in *10 Rillington Place* with a supremely creepy Richard Attenborough in the lead role. Christie was a particularly unsavoury serial killer who murdered for sexual gratification. His *modus operandi* was to lure vulnerable women to his home on the pretence of performing an abortion and sexually assault and strangle them while they were under the influence of gas. He also killed his fellow-tenant's wife and young baby, and when the husband, Timothy Evans, was accused of the murders Christie gave evidence against him. The subsequent hanging of Evans and the later knowledge that Christie was, in fact, responsible galvanised the anti-hanging movement, and public opinion followed suit, eventually forcing its abolition. Dr Simpson was convinced that Christie was responsible for more murders than the eight that are attributed to him. Others disagreed.

In *Forty Years of Murder* Dr Simpson describes the scene that awaited him at Box Copse in the summer of 1948 and the conclusions he was able to draw following the post-mortem on the body:

> I estimated death had taken place eight to ten days previously. I could not be more positive. A newspaper dated 31 July was found in her handbag so this estimate seemed about right.
>
> She had been strangled, probably while lying on her back. I found typical 'fingertip type' bruises in the muscles on both sides of her voice box, and the right upper horn of the hyoid was freshly fractured. There were well-marked signs of asphyxia in the lungs and over the heart. Minor bruises under the scalp and over the spine and hip suggested she had been pressed on her back during the strangling.
>
> The camiknickers and brassiere had become twisted, as by the body sliding finally into the position in which it lay. The stockings were torn, and the skin grazed under the tears. The camiknickers had originally been fastened at the crotch by two buttons. One of these was missing, the thread being torn; how recently was not apparent. The other button was still fastened.
>
> The victim's neatly folded clothes lay about twelve yards from the body, set immediately above the roots of several trees. Near the clothes I noted recent heavy chafing on the lower stems of some of the trees that I thought could have been made by the sliding pressure of footwear, perhaps in resistance to assault or during a struggle and escape downhill. A straight run down ended at the place where the body lay, and if she had been chased down this open track she might well have been thrown or forced on to the ground and strangled on her back.
>
> The tidy removal of most of her clothing suggested she had either stripped to her undies to sunbathe or given approval to some kind of sexual attentions; but the buttoned crotch tie implied that these did not include normal intercourse. Yet there had certainly been penetration of a rough,

forceful kind. I found 'fingertip type' bruises on both thighs, seven more bruises in the muscles around the entrance to the vagina, and a ball of pubic hair at the top of the vagina that could have been carried there only by the insertion of a finger or a penis. The detachment of the hair was further proof of the rough character of the sexual act. The body was too maggot-ridden for swabs for semen, and I could not tell whether or not she had been *virgo intacta* before the assault.

While Dr Simpson was conducting his autopsy, Inspector Narborough and his team were busy checking the Missing Persons reports, and it did not take long before they came to suspect that the body in the mortuary was that of Joan Woodhouse. Police Sergeant Hunter of Lee Road Police Station had made the first connection. There was no identification in the handbag that was found next to the body, but the overlapping front teeth and a detailed description of the clothing and belongings matched various descriptions the police had been given.

Inspector Narborough was conscious that Simpson had estimated the time of death as up to ten days before, and he was anxious that the trail could have gone cold. He concurred with the pathologist's posit that Joan may have been petting with someone she knew when things turned nasty. The folded clothes underpinned this theory, and Narborough's instinct told him her sexual partner would most likely have been the one that Joan had been going to be engaged to and that had caused her such heartache. He decided to brief the press and use them to finger this man immediately, and in the early hours of Thursday morning, 12 August, he made the statement that prompted the *Daily Mail* front page seen earlier. In his haste he did not ensure that Joan's nearest and dearest were fully apprised.

Back in Yorkshire Ida and Annie had begun a long and convoluted bus journey that would take them from their home at 8 Astoria Court, Albion Terrace, Bridlington, to their brother-in-law's house in Barnsley. They were going to have a conference and plan a strategy to find their beloved Joan in the face of what they saw as police indifference. As the bus jogged and shuddered along and early-morning workers boarded on the route, a commuter sat down in front of the women. He unfolded his *Daily Mail*, which in 1948 was a broadsheet, and held it at an angle away from his face so he could get a look at the entire spread. Ida Sheriff gripped the handle in front of her and suppressed a scream. She felt her heart banging within her chest as she absorbed the headline 'Arundel Girl Identified' and saw Joan, her beloved niece, in a familiar family portrait photograph, smiling straight at her.

4
AN INSPECTOR CALLS

Meanwhile, in Arundel, Detective Inspector 'Dixie' Dean interviewed the local man Thomas Stillwell about when and how he had discovered the dead body. The casual labourer and decorator said he had been taking a short cut home from his doctor's surgery when he discovered the body. He mentioned that after finding Joan he saw two young girls playing nearby and he warned them not to go into Box Copse as he did not want them to experience such a grisly sight. He thought he said something about cattle to scare them off. He remembered also asking them where they lived and if they were on holiday. He explained that he had borrowed a bike from the gatekeeper at Swanbourne Lake to ride to the police station. It was a routine witness interview with no real probing. Dean and his team were tidying up the landscape, while Inspector Narborough and his team attended to the bigger picture.

It was Sergeant Bristow, the first officer to see the body after Stillwell had turned up at the police station, however, who experienced the first twinge of unease about the witness when he presented at the police station the following day, Thursday, and asked if a dart had been found at the murder scene. Stillwell explained that he had been at the Black Rabbit to play darts the previous evening (after discovering the body) and had noticed one was missing, and casting his mind back, believed it must have fallen out of his pocket when he discovered the body and had bent over. Sergeant Bristow confirmed that a dart had indeed been found.

Experienced and dogged, Fred Narborough was elsewhere pursuing his line of inquiry with gusto. He explained his train of thought later in his autobiography *Murder On My Mind*:

So a girl who claimed she intended visiting her father in Yorkshire is found dead in Sussex beside a pile of outer clothing, neatly folded after removal. Her diary lists page after page of men's names. The mental picture conjured up from the available evidence grows into sharper focus: August Bank Holiday weekend. A girl and a man travel together to Worthing or meet by arrangement in the seaside resort. The girl leaves her suitcase at the left-luggage office and the couple find local accommodation. They visit Arundel Park in the brilliant sunshine and choose Box Copse for their lovemaking. Of all the clothing on the half-naked body, only a shoulder-strap is torn, but she has been raped and strangled.

Any amateur criminologist could have told me the next step in the investigation. Locate close men friends of Joan Woodhouse and find out where they were during the holiday weekend. Of course!

The press, as well as the police, seized on Joan's address book and the 'one hundred-plus men's names listed' and, over the coming days, media insinuations were made that Joan was a nymphomaniac or, worse still, a prostitute. The term 'good-time girl' was used at the time as a catch-all for girls who were considered to have loose morals by people who believed they occupied a higher moral ground. Indeed, there was a film showing at the cinemas at this very time called *Good-Time Girl*, based on an Arthur La Bern book *Night Darkens The Street*. These slurs heaped misery on top of utter despair for John Woodhouse and his sisters-in-law. As devout Christians they found this media violation of her character almost as painful as the murderous violation of her body. They pleaded with Inspector Narborough to refute these suggestions publicly and assured him he was on the wrong track in pursuing this line of inquiry. Joan was pure and sensible. She would never have consented to intercourse or intimate relations with a man she was not married to. She could not lie either. It was against her religion. To arrange a secret assignation with a man would be unthinkable.

Fred Narborough, in his defence, was a hardened, worldly-wise copper. He had seen it all. The number of parents he had dealt with over the course of his career who believed that their son or their daughter was an angel, when the reality was that they were sleeping around or out at night burgling houses or something more serious, was mind boggling. One thing his police life had taught him was that nobody really knows anyone. Secret lives are legion. We only think they are rare because only a few of those secret lives ever come to light. Cynicism, inevitably, has to be an important tool in the detective's kit. He was sure that the murderer's identity was in his hands, quite literally, in Joan's address book in her neat, meticulous handwriting. They would have their man as they eliminated the names one by one. The briefing to the press was intended to accelerate that process.

Maintaining the press momentum was uppermost in Narborough's mind when he arranged for the wife of an Arundel police sergeant to dress in identical clothes to the ones that Joan was wearing on that fateful day and then have Police Sergeant Brown, the official photographer from Chichester Police, superimpose an image of Joan's face on the body. He circulated this to the newspapers and news agencies along with an appeal for information, and it duly appeared in most national and local titles on Friday 13 August. Despite the superstitious date he was confident this would result in a stream of eye witnesses.

Over the weekend it became apparent that the sweep of hotels and guest houses in Worthing had turned up nothing. Archie Greenshields, then a young policeman in Littlehampton, remembers:

On attending the police station that day I discovered that there was a tremendous hive of activity. Not long afterwards I was sent with others to assist inquiries that pointed to the fact she had been in Worthing.

Each of us from the Littlehampton and Arundel Division were to work with a member of the Worthing Borough team. Armed with a recent photo of the girl, Joan Woodhouse, we were told to visit every hotel in Worthing in an attempt to discover where she had been staying. I worked with a Detective Constable Stoddard, who subsequently reached the rank of Chief Inspector, and we had the task of visiting each hotel on Marine Parade from the pier westwards.

On top of this the results from contacting the men listed in Joan's address book served to puncture further Narborough's confidence in achieving an early resolution to the case. It now transpired that Joan was the unofficial secretary of a librarians' professional association, and each of the men (and women) listed were fellow librarians. Nevertheless, each and every person in the book would have to be spoken to and eliminated from the inquiry, just in case the murderer *was* lurking in those pages. It did mean, though, that the inspector now began to listen more attentively to Mr Woodhouse and Joan's aunts about the kind of girl Joan Woodhouse actually had been.

The man Narborough had been pinning most of his hopes on, the man who knew Joan well and was referred to in the *Daily Mail* article, was located in Folkestone, Kent, and the inspector visited him personally along with an Inspector Hoare of Worthing Police. It was Ted Roberts, who was now the assistant librarian at the public library in the seaside town. He explained that he had met Joan in 1946 when they were both students at University College, London. He confirmed that he had been romantically linked to Joan but had not seen her since the Easter weekend four months earlier, when they had both stayed with his mother at Flintshire. He said they had arranged to meet in May when he was addressing a conference in Scarborough, Yorkshire, but Joan never arrived. Because of this he elected not to visit her in Bridlington where she was staying with her aunts. The intervals between exchanges of letters between them lengthened. Crucially, even though the policeman was already suitably impressed with his intelligence, status and character, Ted Roberts could prove he was hiking on the weekend of Joan's murder some one hundred miles away from Arundel. Narborough had to accept that Roberts was definitely not his man.

On 12 August the *Daily Express* had also tracked down an increasingly uncomfortable Roberts, and he had told them he thought that Joan may have been suffering from 'post-war neurosis'. He very politely referred to her at all times in the interview as 'Miss Woodhouse'. The *Express* also located other contacts of Joan, one being an unnamed porter at the YWCA who volunteered the information that Joan had the nickname Splinters and claimed she had spoken to him of another romantic interest, a man named John. Finally, unhelpfully and sensationally, the newspaper raised the spectre of some sort of murderous vendetta against librarians, pointing to the recent murders of Barbara Shuttleworth, who worked in the House of Commons Library, and Margaret Whiteside, a Liverpool librarian. It seemed irrelevant to these barrel-scraping, story-seeking hacks that two separate men had already been charged with these crimes.

For a fleeting moment on the Thursday the possibility of a murder–suicide presented itself. Police were diverted from searching Arundel Park for clues to the River Arun where an angler had reported seeing a man's body in the water. This was on a spot between Wepham and Burpham about a mile from the murder scene, but although police dragged the river as the tide rose no body was ever recovered.

Fred Narborough stepped up his investigation, marshalling all the resources available to him in this little pocket of southern England. His team compiled a list of every unattached male living in Worthing on the bank-holiday weekend, and then widened the area to Arundel and the surrounding villages. Each man was questioned about his activities over the weekend and asked whether they had entered Arundel Park. Presumably the police were under the impression that a propensity to sexual violence did not extend to married men.

In addition, holiday-makers in Worthing and Arundel, now long departed, were traced and questioned. Employees of British Rail at Victoria, Worthing and Arundel were interviewed, as were coach and taxi-drivers. Later, every male, married or not, over the age of fifteen and living in Arundel was subjected to more intense probing over their movements. The inspector's belief and hope that he would have made an arrest by Friday was not to become reality.

The inquest opened on the Friday at the town hall, and Mr FW Butler, the coroner for Horsham, promptly adjourned. The man who found the body, Thomas Stillwell, attended in case he was required as a witness. When the hearing closed he approached Sergeant Bristow and asked if he could point out the murdered girl's family so he could express his condolences. This the sergeant did, and he watched Stillwell approach John Woodhouse and Ida Sheriff. Ida later recalled the moment, saying she felt that something wasn't right. She told Lena Bamber that Stillwell was not discreet in offering his condolences and stood among them a little bit too long. John Woodhouse kept his counsel. He had confidence and trust in the English police and the age-old, tried-and-tested legal system. They knew what they were doing, he was sure. He hoped.

5
A SUSPECT

Inspector Narborough knew all too well that if a case is not cracked in the first few days then, as each additional day passes, the trail gets colder, and unless there is a lucky breakthrough the murderer's chances of eluding the police increase dramatically.

Ted Roberts had claimed to the police that Joan had had a passionate love affair with a friend of her father's. He said that Joan had confided in him that she'd had intercourse with this older man. This second man, who was living in Edinburgh, absolutely denied any intimacy with Joan and, crucially for the detective, could prove he was five hundred miles away from Box Copse on 31 July and had not seen Joan for a year. The claim is mentioned in police files, and this author has found no other record of it. It is at odds with Roberts' reason for calling off the engagement, which he said was because of Joan's deep religious convictions. The allegation is also at odds with the family's claims about Joan's romantic life.

A female librarian colleague and friend of Joan's was interviewed by police, and she was able to confirm that Joan had been intensely involved with Ted Roberts. She said that he was low church, and this caused Joan much vexation so she had sought the counsel of her spiritual adviser. This man of the church had apparently expressed horror at Joan marrying Ted or altering her religion to accommodate him, and it was this that had launched Joan into depression. This friend was very concerned about Joan and had also urged her to move to the YWCA hostel. She had only moved to Blackheath as recently as 4 July. The friend had asked a mutual male friend to keep an eye on Joan when she went off for her summer holidays. Narborough thought he might be on to something here, but this man could also prove he was elsewhere on 29 July and had not seen Joan since the 25th.

A Bognor postman came forward and said he remembered delivering two letters with a London postmark addressed to Miss Joan Woodhouse, c/o The Sussex Club, Middleton, Sussex. Middleton is on the coast about six miles from Arundel. This was on Friday 13 August. Only after he had delivered them did his mind make the connection, and he took it upon himself to inquire at the club the following day while on his round. Strangely, the letters had disappeared, and there was no member of this club sharing Joan's name, so he reported the matter to the police. It was a perplexing development but not one that the police could discover anything further about.

More dead ends followed as a swathe of sightings generated by the mock-up picture of Joan in the press flooded into the murder headquarters set up in the little Arundel Police Station. One woman thought she had directed Joan to the Warming Pan restaurant in Arundel when she had apparently asked where she could get a cup of coffee. A courting couple had been in Arundel Park at about 5.30 p.m. when they saw a man emerge from some bushes after they had heard twigs breaking and scuffling. He apparently sat down under a tree and stared at them for about thirty minutes before walking off. Another man from Worthing had been driving away from the Black Rabbit after closing time on Saturday night when he saw a man walking hurriedly towards his car and then hiding behind some road-mending equipment. Leslie Grant, licensee of the George And Dragon in nearby Burpham, was convinced a woman wearing the same distinctive dress as Joan had been in the private bar of his pub on the bank-holiday Saturday with a man. He even overheard their conversation about walking to Arundel. Other sightings – more easily dismissed – came from Littlehampton, Brighton, Worthing and Bognor. The investigation was going nowhere fast.

Much was made in the media of the 'revelation' that Joan had attended a party in north London on 13 July. Papers reported that police believed Joan made her arrangements for her visit to Arundel at this party. The stories about this, in the papers of 2 September, were obviously triggered by briefings from Inspector Narborough, who urged anybody who had attended the party to come forward. One suspects Narborough was bluffing or flying a kite. The party was barely mentioned again, and surely if someone had overheard any Arundel arrangements being made at this party such evidence would have been referred to later at the various hearings. It never was. The Woodhouse family viewed the development as irrelevant and scurrilous – a further implication that Joan was some sort of party girl.

Local police had their noses closer to the ground than the Yard team and were better attuned to the feelings, opinions and gossip in Arundel. It was a steady flow of whispered comments, innuendo and asides about Thomas Stillwell that prompted Detective Inspector Dean of West Sussex CID to call him into the police station again and take a lengthy statement for the first time in the inquiry, on Thursday 19 August, more than a week after the discovery of the body. Dean was coming at this interview from the point of view of testing an alibi and not to gather a witness statement now. He may well have been nudged in that direction by Sergeant Bristow.

Thomas Stillwell was born in Arundel in 1924 and was well known in the town. There have been Stillwells in Arundel and its environs for almost as long as the castle – one family-history researcher claims to have traced Thomas's paternal line back to the sixteenth century. The boy's father was Thomas Rawlins Stillwell, born around 1879, who spent a long spell in the Royal Navy before returning to Arundel and taking on labouring work to supplement his naval pension. In 1923 he married 21-year-old Ellen Agnes Parsons. Ellen had spent part of her childhood in a public house. In 1911 she was living in the White Horse on Arundel's Tarrant Street, where her father was the licensee. She was nearly half Thomas Rawlins' age and had already had an illegitimate daughter, born in 1919, when she was seventeen. Thomas Rawlins is named as the father on the daughter's birth certificate. Ellen's mother, Agnes, had been present at the birth in a cottage in Offham called Foxes' Oven. A son, Peter, had been born the previous year to Thomas, and young Thomas came along on 30 June 1924 followed by his brother Arthur in 1927.

In police records Thomas Rawlins Stillwell is described as 'a man sodden in drink' and 'of no use as a witness'. The police also observed that any reflections of his on young Thomas Stillwell should be taken lightly, as he did not like the boy because he did not believe he was his biological father. Indeed, according to the police notes, the parentage of all the children was in doubt, and the relationship between Thomas Rawlins and his family was a turbulent one. Older brother Peter left the family home shortly after the spotlight fell on his younger brother. The police files note that Peter had lost a hand during the Second World War and that they believed he was a thoroughly decent and trustworthy individual.

Young Thomas had been a butcher's boy during the war, delivering food around the local area on his bicycle. It is not known why Stillwell did not serve himself, as he would have been twenty-one years old when the war ended. As the boy grew older and stronger he became a general labourer, turning his hand to house-painting, quarry work and asphalting, and was generally gainfully employed.

He was also an enthusiastic footballer and played for a time for Arundel Football Club – an amateur team of reasonable standard – and at other times he turned out for nearby Rustington FC. Some press reports of the time claimed that Stillwell was of such a standard that professional football clubs had expressed some interest in seeing him play.

The Stillwells lived in Foxes' Oven, a tied cottage owned by the Duke of Norfolk. The small red-bricked dwelling was in Offham, a tiny hamlet at the top of Mill Road passing the Black Rabbit on the right-hand side. The family's meagre household income was supplemented by the occasional discreet poaching of rabbits and other game from the land around them.

In a novel published in 2002, *Foxes' Oven* by Michael de Larrabeiti, the author writes about a young girl evacuated to a cottage called Foxes' Oven in Offham near Arundel in 1940. The author himself had been evacuated to Arundel during the war, and one assumes the following description was based on his own experience:

Then the path became so steep that there were steps cut into it, the risers made with pegs and strips of osier. There was a banister too, a length of sturdy branch nailed into living tree trunks, worn smooth by the caress of human hands. The steps twisted to the left and dropped under the bulge of the hillside, and, where there were gaps in the foliage, I caught the play of silver in the pale twilight that lay to the north, shallow ditches in a vast plain, and beyond that, the broad sweep of the Arun in the distance. It was hard for me to believe that people really lived here: it was the wood at the end of the world.

The path twisted again and dropped down to a flatness. The branches thinned and I could see further – a wisp of smoke, stately as a column, rising from a chimney; then a wooden gate, lopsided and open; a low fence. A roof gleamed under the trees that leant over it, twigs touching the moss-stained tiles. What light there was glimmered only faintly and lingered near the ground in shallow pools.

Not a leaf moved, there was no breeze, only a scowling silence. The windows of the house were blind, no lamps shining in them; there were no early stars in the sky, and no moon. It was a dark place holding onto its last breath, and the strangeness of it invaded my heart, and emptied it. I missed my footing and stumbled, slipping to the ground, sinking easily, letting go of the basket and Agnes' best coat. It was a defeat and I knew it was, and the scalding tears poured down my face and my sobs hurt me. Agnes looked over her shoulder, without a word, unwilling or unable to come to my assistance, holding, as she was, the other basket and the other stick of dead rabbits. I lay on my back, without a shred of hope left in me. I started up at the dark sky and let the tears go . . . and that was how I came to Foxes' Oven.

Surprisingly, at the second, more intense interview, Stillwell could not be sure about his precise movements on the bank-holiday Saturday, the estimated day of the murder, but thought he 'might' have painted the outside of his house in the morning, 'might' have shopped in Arundel, too, and 'might' have gone to Littlehampton in the afternoon. He 'thought' he had gone to the pictures in the evening. He usually did. Turning to the day he discovered the body Stillwell reiterated that he was taking a short cut home from the doctor's surgery where he had been to have a poisoned hand looked at. Someone in that interview room knew that Box Copse was not, by any stretch of the imagination, a short cut between Stillwell's doctor and his house. At this interview he does not appear to have been pressed on this, but the discrepancy and growing doubt about the local man's story was passed on to Inspector Narborough.

The Scotland Yard detective, despite being led up a succession of blind alleys, was still convinced that Joan's private (maybe secret) life would be the key to unlocking the case, and his focus and head was still in that space. Narborough was now, though, in a dialogue with Ida Sheriff, who seemed to know the girl's character best of all. Ida had forwarded him letters that Joan had written in which she talked about her planned engagement to Ted Roberts and her feelings of hopelessness when the relationship fell apart. The aunt constantly reiterated Joan's good character and urged the policeman to abandon the notion that her niece was capable of going off with a strange man willingly or that she had a relationship that she did not know about. Joan told them everything, she stressed.

Ida's letters to Narborough during these early weeks indicate that she was reaching the conclusion that Joan had taken her own life. She asked the inspector if she could see the reported religious material found in Joan's handbag, as she wanted to know 'what comfort she was taking at the end'. This train of thought flew in the face of the evidence that she was murdered and can only be explained by the aunt's *wish* for it to be suicide at this stage in preference to a brutal, sexual murder. It was easier to deal with. This was a family in deep shock.

An article in the *Daily Express* of 21 August 1948, which must have been based on some measure of police briefing, gives an idea of where Narborough was focusing his inquiry. The paper said that the man who was seen with Joan Woodhouse on the day she was strangled in Arundel Castle grounds on 31 July may have had his brownish hair artificially waved. The *Express* continued by saying it was the latest clue obtained by Scotland Yard and West Sussex detectives investigating the murder. According to the article, the police knew that the man was between thirty and forty, of medium height and build and with a cultured voice. The article went on to reference Joan's diary, containing '150 names of relatives and friends and an address book at Lee Green YWCA hostel, where she lodged'. The article ended with a tantalising: 'The Yard has also put all available officers on to the London hunt for Joan's girlfriend believed to be withholding vital information. They now think she may need police protection before she will speak.'

The final sentence raises more questions. Who was this girlfriend of Joan's who was believed to be withholding information? Was the *Express* getting carried away, or had the police briefed the press on another lead? No further references can be found to the friend or the vital information she was harbouring, and the statement has to be put down as one of the many red herrings and dead ends that pepper the entire case and investigation.

This was just the sort of article that was unsettling the family so. The police were obviously treating the alleged sighting at the George And Dragon as definite, even though Joan's aunts and father were sceptical that Joan would be meeting any man, let alone going into a pub with him. More damaging to Joan's character and the direction of the investigation was the innuendo around the address book, the diary, the 150 names and the mysterious girlfriend who might need police protection. It all conjured up images of Joan inhabiting some shady, seedy, secret world that the family was convinced was absurd and plain wrong.

On Monday 23 August 1948, nearly a fortnight after taking on the case, Fred Narborough came face to face with Thomas Stillwell for the very first time. The detective decided to get the measure of this man who was featuring heavily in local gossip and clear up the discrepancy about why he was at Box Copse on 10 August. When the seasoned copper challenged Stillwell about his 'short cut' claim he became very agitated. It was the first time that he had been seriously challenged about anything he had said. This was also the first occasion when he realised that the police did not necessarily believe everything he claimed.

'I will tell you the truth,' he suddenly declared.

Narborough and Detective Inspector Dean looked at each other and then at Stillwell. Was this going to be an unexpected breakthrough? Momentarily the two policemen were excited, utterly attuned to what the man was preparing to say.

'I was at Box Copse looking for rabbits,' he began. 'I was punching through the brush to flush a rabbit out. It's poaching, it is. And if I admit to that then my parents could lose their cottage. That's why I lied. It's forbidden to take rabbits off the Duke's land.'

Narborough was a country boy himself. He recognised this man in front of him. He'd grown up himself catching or trying to catch rabbits, dipping his hand into birds' nests to take the eggs, catching fish from the rivers and lakes and, as a farmer, shooting game, raptors and crows. Landowners and those who worked it had coexisted for centuries, the workers showing deference outwardly but covertly supplementing their existence with the fruit of their master's land. It was custom and practice stretching back to feudal times. Landowners and agricultural labourers. Gamekeepers and poachers. Stillwell seemed genuinely distressed about the disaster he could potentially wreak upon his family. The Scotland Yard man could perfectly understand why this simple, young countryman would lie. Another investigative cul-de-sac? Inspector Fred Narborough was satisfied. Back to the grindstone.

If Narborough had been more circumspect he might have asked how

Stillwell intended to catch a rabbit with no equipment, no nets. Even country people find it difficult to flush out, catch and kill a rabbit with no ferret, no nets, no nothing – with bare hands. And Stillwell's bare hands were infected – or one of them was; that was the reason he had been to the doctor. Narborough clearly missed an opportunity to prise open Stillwell's story here, but he was still not seeing the down-to-earth country lad in front of him as a serious suspect, something he would live to regret.

6
A MOMENT OF CLARITY

As September fell away leads were drying up, and anybody and everybody who had a known connection to Joan Woodhouse had now been fully eliminated from police inquiries. The initial press interest in the murder had waned. On Monday 27 September Inspector Narborough called a day-long conference in which the detectives from London and Sussex locked themselves in a room amid a fog of cigarette-smoke and brainstormed for several hours. It was decided to invite Ida Sheriff down to London and go through Joan's life from cradle to Box Copse one last time, face-to-face, before the murderer-was-someone-she-knew line of inquiry was finally abandoned. Narborough picked up the phone and extended the invitation to Ida.

'Anything to find that beast,' she replied. Clearly, Ida had now moved away from her suicide conclusion.

In *Murder On My Mind* Fred Narborough claims it was the meeting with Ida, which began at 10 a.m. on Wednesday 29 September, that was the turning point in the investigation. Mrs Sheriff arrived with her sister Annie Blades and her sister-in-law, a Mrs Johnson. He encouraged them to recount Joan's life once more, and Ida did so with occasional interjections from the other two ladies.

First, the interview nailed the perplexing issue of why Joan would go to Arundel in the first place. The three women stressed how the two sisters had lived in Worthing some years earlier and had visited Arundel with Joan many times, picnicking on the slope down from Box Copse. It had been a favourite spot and held happy childhood memories for Joan. Ida was bemused at the police's treatment of this information as new, as she was sure she had told Narborough and others on the telephone and thought she had put this in letters to him. Indeed, in one letter she asked

Narborough why the newspapers were allowed to continue saying it was a mystery why Joan travelled to Arundel when to the family it was not.

It was the second 'revelation', though, that electrified the interview room.

'She was a normal, healthy, good-living girl with a very happy disposition,' continued Ida. 'She loved outdoor life and almost worshipped the sun. At the first blink of real sunshine she would strip off her outside clothing and lie down.'

Narborough and his Yard colleague, an Inspector Hatherill, jumped to their feet. (George Hatherill, not specifically on this investigation, was a very significant player within Scotland Yard. He is credited with forming Special Branch and would soon work on the John Christie, 10 Rillington Place murders. He was awarded the OBE in 1954 and ended his career with a flourish in 1964 when he led the investigation into the Great Train Robbery.)

'Have I said something wrong?' asked Ida, nonplussed at the extreme reaction.

'No, ma'am,' Narborough said, 'but you didn't tell us this early enough.'

The aunt elaborated. Joan sunbathed at every opportunity, in the back garden of her home or in a secluded spot in the country. If there was any sun she would remove her frock and lay down. Inspector Hatherill gently but firmly asked Ida why she had not mentioned this before. Ida became distressed and could only say she was so terribly upset.

In *Murder On My Mind* Fred Narborough clearly marks this as the moment of 'clarity', and it is implied that he blamed the family for not divulging this habit of Joan's earlier and therefore impeding the investigation and allowing the real trail to go cold:

I felt like beating my head against the wall. With a single sentence the widow had destroyed a most promising theory. Joan Woodhouse had journeyed to Arundel alone. The events of the fatal Saturday became clear. The clarity mocked the six wasted weeks during which we hunted a shadowy male companion who had never existed.

The girl must have turned away from the bustling crowds at King's Cross station, thinking with nostalgia of the peaceful Sussex countryside. Maybe she did not want to face the familiar surroundings at home, where she had battled with her feelings over the shattered love affair.

59

I recalled a remark by her former sweetheart, so significant now. Joan, he had said, hated carrying luggage and would deposit this at the first opportunity. That brought us as far as the Worthing cloakroom.

In Arundel the statements from the Wren and the chemist put her progress towards the park as sometime after two o' clock.

Instead of seeking a secluded spot for love-making, she had gone straight to Box Copse, which she knew.

She must have eased her frock over her head, then neatly folded the garment to add it to the tidy, growing pile of possessions by her side. The string of pearls would have been unclasped so that the evenness of the sun tan around the throat would not be ruined, the slender throat that was later to feel the brutal grip of the murderer's spanning hands.

She would have laid down full-length upon her coat and surrendered her body to the warmth of the afternoon sun.

The moment of rape, or of rape and murder at possibly the same instant – the pathologist's report stressed the fracture of the right upper horn on the voice box – must have been between three o'clock and six o'clock that Saturday.

The sauntering afternoon-in-the-hot-sun walk of a girl seeking the seclusion of Box Copse from the High Street had been paced out many times.

Joan Woodhouse must have reached her last-but-one resting place in the full heat of the day.

Maybe she stirred at times, elbowed herself up to finish the bottle of thirst-quencher.

The full heat of the sun disappeared around six o'clock. Sometime before that she was dead, murdered. As the earth chilled so did her ravished body.

A man tormented by his sexual desires must have glimpsed the near-naked girl, innocently sunning in the lonely clearing. His lust had been too much for him.

Maybe the victim had been asleep when he pounced, smothering her by his weight. There was enough evidence that she had tried to escape, until the hot hands had squeezed her life away.

All must have been over very quickly.

Inspector Narborough clearly dates this explosive moment as being Wednesday 29 September, leading his readers to believe that when this revelation was made it was only then that they started looking for 'a man tormented by his sexual desires', yet as far back as 7 September a possible candidate for such a person had broken cover – Tom Stillwell.

In addition, family members and friends were adamant that Joan's connections to Arundel had been explained to the police many times and that was why they were becoming increasingly frustrated at the police's inability to stop misinformation appearing repeatedly in the national press. Some commented it was as if Narborough had his theory and did not want to entertain information that clashed with it. His comment – 'with a single sentence the widow had destroyed a most promising theory' – seems to support this.

Lena Bamber said in 2010 that when she spoke to the police back in 1948 she was quite clear in her mind how Joan had ended up in Arundel and she, too, could not understand why they chose to ignore her.

I told Mr Narborough that Joan would have fully intended to catch the 10.10 a.m. from Kings Cross. I'm sure she crossed London with great diffi-culty because of the unprecedented crowds in town for the Olympics and would have decided at some point to give up on the idea and decided to catch the night-train as she sometimes did. Therefore she had a day to kill, and that is when she decided to visit Arundel. I can remember her saying not long before she had had to put off a trip to Arundel with her aunts because of not being able to get the petrol due to rationing. I think she went there so she could say to Nida and Nan when she got to Yorkshire – guess where I've been? Box Copse! I really think so.

And I can also vouch for those crowds that Saturday morning because I was there. I came in the other direction into King's Cross from Derbyshire with my brother Harry who I was taking to the games, and King's Cross was a sea of people. And with the heat it was unbearable. People were passing out. We watched as the porters pushed one woman through the window of a train door because the door could not be opened. I have never seen crowds like it before or since.

David Kynaston, in his excellent book *Austerity Britain*, throws more light on the travel situation at London mainline stations on that oppressively hot day. He says that large queues snaked back from the main London railway stations, and extra trains took day-trippers and holiday-makers to the seaside. From Victoria 25,700 travelled to the Kent coast and 63,287 to Eastbourne and Bognor.

This paints a picture of a truly chaotic and stressful day on the London railway network and lends weight to Lena Bamber's theory on Joan's thinking that extraordinary morning. She may well have abandoned the frightening prospect of cramming on to dangerous Underground platforms and squeezing into overloaded carriages in order to reach King's Cross. A train to Arundel and the relative peace until the crowds had subsided could have seemed a very sensible idea.

Perhaps Inspector Narborough could ignore what Joan's family and friends were telling him, but there was no way he could dismiss what Detective Inspector Dean and his own Sergeant Pattison had to say after their next session with Thomas Stillwell.

7
DOUBTING THOMAS

Why, specifically, Detective Inspector Dean and Sergeant Pattison had Stillwell in again is not clear. One of Ida Sheriff's letters to the Director of Public Prosecutions (DPP) later refers to a rift between the Sussex detectives and Scotland Yard and a particular incident when windows had to be closed at the police station after arguments became heated and passing pedestrians were seen eavesdropping. This may have been at the brainstorming session. Ida implies that West Sussex police believed there was a strong case to charge the local man and Scotland Yard did not. It is possible that Dean was by now very suspicious of Stillwell, and while Inspector Narborough was ploughing other furrows he had him back and insisted that Sergeant Pattison, Narborough's right-hand man from the Yard, join him in the interrogation.

A former resident of some railway cottages at nearby Yapton, then only a girl, remembered in 2010 the police coming to arrest Stillwell, who was at the time working for a contractor to the Southern Railway, repainting their properties. This lady remembers it well because her family had just had cause to remonstrate with Stillwell's employer as the young painter had been sexually harassing a young aunt that had been staying with them.

This interview was extraordinarily revelatory. Stillwell admitted to being in Arundel Park not just on the day he found the body but on 31 July, the day that Joan was most likely murdered. He also volunteered that he had been sexually aroused in the park on that first day and had masturbated behind a bush. He said that he had whistled at a girl and when she had ignored him and walked past he had muttered 'Bugger you, then'. He said he had watched and followed her for a time. The two policemen were dumbfounded. They calmly pushed him to say more. Stillwell appeared to be struggling with his emotions and Sergeant Pattison produced a photograph of Joan and placed it in front of him.

'Is this the girl you spoke to on Saturday 31 July?'

Stillwell agreed it was and started to cry. Both policemen fully expected and hoped that a full and detailed confession would now follow.

'I suppose I am to blame for her death,' he sobbed tantalisingly.

'Why do you say that, Tom?' pressed Detective Inspector Dean carefully. The anticipation in the room was palpable.

Stillwell stopped himself and remained silent for some hanging seconds before saying, 'Well, it was me who scared her, and she ran into Box Copse where someone must have found her.'

A pregnant silence ensued. The policemen, anxious not to spook their suspect, waited for the man to say more.

Stillwell appeared to be composing himself. 'Let me look at the picture again.'

Dean passed it over, and Stillwell studied it carefully and then handed it back, 'No, thinking about it, that picture does not resemble the girl I saw at all.'

The moment had passed. The possible tipping point gone. Never again was Stillwell so open with the police, and afterwards only back-pedalled from the potentially incriminating point he had reached.

If this interview prompted a belated search of Stillwell's house and the removal of his clothes and shoes it is not recorded anywhere. Some of Joan's clothing has been preserved and has been examined in recent years under cold-case schemes. There has been no reference to any of Stillwell's clothing being kept. The Woodhouse family claim there was no immediate attempt after this interview to gather potential forensic evidence from Stillwell, and to them and others that is one of the key mysteries to the case.

In police files seen by the author a detective's report states that clothing from Stillwell *was* examined but no evidence was found. The family felt that his boots would have been particularly interesting bearing in mind the marks on the tree at Box Copse recorded by Professor Keith Simpson. If Stillwell *were* the murderer of Joan Woodhouse then it is likely that given the length of time between the murder and his arrest any clothing vulnerable to detection would have been disposed of.

The Woodhouse family were also scathing about the length of time it took to reach this point. It was now nearly seven weeks after the murder. Clues had been lost. What doctor did Stillwell see on the day of the discovery of Joan's body? What was the injury to his hand? He said he had a poisoned finger. If this had been examined on 10 or 11 August when Stillwell went to the police then it might have been possible to confirm or discount whether that injury had resulted from a human bite. If it had, it might well have been possible to discern by teeth patterns whether that bite was from Joan. The second police report refers to the doctor being seen but it is not clear whether this was in the Narborough investigation or the later one.

It is bizarre that Stillwell did not come under immediate sharp scrutiny when he first reported his macabre discovery. Followers of the true-crime genre and viewers of detective and crime TV programmes will know that the first people to eliminate from a murder inquiry are normally the next of kin, the last known person to see the victim alive and/or the person who found them. Inspector Narborough's dogged pursuit of a lover of Joan's to the detriment of other lines of inquiry was, as he admitted himself, a major failing, although he did not publicly take the blame for this.

Relations between the Woodhouse family and Inspector Narborough had not yet become strained. On 8 October Ida Sheriff wrote a long letter to the policeman, warmly thanking him for his 'courtesy and care' on their recent visit to London. No mention is made of Stillwell or any suspect so one can assume the family had not yet been fully informed of the developments on that front. Instead, the aunt is mainly concerned with the negative inferences about Joan's character that continued to colour the press coverage. Again, she urged Narborough to rectify this. She wanted the newspapers to stress Joan's good character and detail her Rule of Life. Not only was Joan's character under attack but people were less likely to come forward if they thought Joan was 'that sort of girl', they argued with some justification.

On Saturday 9 October Detective Inspector Dean again interviewed Thomas Stillwell. Yet more was revealed. Perhaps Dean had some more evidence to confront him with. Whatever the reason, Stillwell now remembered he went to Littlehampton in the late afternoon of 31 July to buy a new shirt. Hepworths, the men's retailer in the nearby seaside town, confirmed a sale of such a shirt around the time Stillwell said he had been there. He does not appear to have been pressed as to why he needed a new shirt and why he did not purchase one in Arundel. At one point Stillwell looked earnestly at the policemen and said, 'I know all the facts point to me, but I am innocent.'

Again the suspect was released.

Inspector Narborough finally stepped in and had Stillwell in for a marathon session on Tuesday 19 October from 9.40 a.m. to 5.15 p.m. and then again on Wednesday 20 October from 6.30 p.m. to 5.30 a.m. The intensity and unsocial hours were designed to break him down once and for all. These interviews revealed that Stillwell's previous admission to masturbating behind a bush on 31 July was not a one-off aberration. He refers to the bush incident once more but also volunteers that he became aroused again by a group of Girl Guides on that very same day. He says he lay down on his side and 'made water'. It is a strange term and could perhaps have been substituted for something else Stillwell had said by the policeman who wrote up the statement in a desire to make the words more palatable for public consumption. It has been suggested to the author that he could have been referring to urinating, but it is highly unusual for some-body to lay down on their side to urinate, and in the context of what else had been said it is certain he is referring to masturbation and ejaculation.

Stillwell also made the astonishing admission that his sole purpose for entering Arundel Park that Saturday was to 'show himself off to two young girls' he had seen. He added that, on the day of discovering the body when he had seen the two young girls near the body and warned them away, he had considered exposing himself to them in order to scare them off. He was not sure if he had or not. This would suggest he was exposing his erect penis so much he could not be positive exactly when, where and to whom.

Questions about the type of man he was aside, who on just finding a dead body would be able to consider exposing himself to two young girls? Does this not make nonsense of his claim to be shocked and upset and his rush to pedal furiously to the police station? By his own admission he also asked the girls where they were from and whether they were on their holidays. Would anyone be able to frame such a casual conversation minutes after discovering a decomposing corpse of a near-naked young woman?

As mitigating circumstances for this bizarre behaviour Stillwell cited the fact that he had recently split from his girlfriend and was sexually frustrated. He elaborated on his sex life with this lady saying he suffered from premature ejaculation but proudly boasted of his ability to gain an erection again almost immediately. He said that when he did manage intercourse he always withdrew and ejaculated into a handkerchief. The police had not pressed for this information, and in writing up their report they commented that Stillwell seemed conceited about his sexual prowess and appetite.

Here was a man who not only 'discovered' the body but also admitted to being in the immediate vicinity on the day of the murder, had no alibi placing him anywhere else at the actual time of the murder *and* had a motive – he was a sexual predator who lacked control and became easily aroused by women and young girls and, by his own admission, stalked them.

The evidence, although seductive, was circumstantial, and because of the time lapse forensic proof was now going to be unlikely to emerge. Narborough knew that some might take the view that he had mishandled the inquiry and it was his fault that the crucial evidence was now not available. His intense grilling, while revealing much, had not yielded a confession, so he decided that he would have to sit and wait for Stillwell to slip up by way of admitting his guilt elsewhere or some other means before he could lay charges.

He rang Ida Sheriff and John Woodhouse and said, 'We know who the man is. He knows we know who he is. We don't have enough evidence yet. It is just a matter of time before we put our hand on his shoulder. Rest assured.'

The family were by now not surprised to be told that that man was Thomas Stillwell. The man who had discovered the body. The man who had approached them after the inquest to express his sorrow at their loss. The man who had caused them to feel a chill when he had attempted to open up a conversation with them after expressing those condolences.

8
PERSON UNKNOWN

The Coroner for Horsham, Mr FW Butler, an incredible eighty-nine years old (when the average male lifespan was seventy or under), opened the inquest at Arundel Town Hall on Monday morning, 22 November 1948. He was fifty years into the job. A *Sussex Express* report of 19 March 1901 has him officiating as coroner for West Sussex in the case of a Nuthurst farmer who shot himself while in a depressed state. The inquest indicated that the slip-up by Thomas Stillwell on which Inspector Narborough was pinning his hopes had not occurred. No Scotland Yard leather-gloved hand had clamped on to any shoulder in the previous month.

'This is the adjournment from the inquest, which I conducted on the 13 August last on the body of the girl who was found dead in Arundel Park,' Mr Butler began. 'I took evidence of identity in order that the burial might take place and adjourned the inquest *sine die* in order that inquiries might be made. That was three months ago.

'At the moment nothing definite has been obtained as a result of those inquiries, but the case is still alive, I may say, and will be continued although three months has elapsed, and I think it is time that the death certificate should be issued for registration purposes.

'This girl had not been seen since 31 July last, and it appears apparent that she came down to Worthing and then came to Arundel. There is evidence that she was familiar with Arundel Park and was fond of going there and had been there on several occasions before with an aunt of hers. She was also, sometimes at any rate, given to sunbathing, and there is evidence there was foul play apparently here. Dr Hunt was present when a post-mortem examination was performed by the official pathologist. He will show you and satisfy you, I am sure, that there was foul play – that the girl met with her death – that she was murdered, in fact – I am sure you will be satisfied of it.'

The three solicitors then introduced themselves: Mr Falconer for the family of Joan Woodhouse, Mr Porter for the police and Mr Vincent Jackson for the witness Thomas Philip George Stillwell. There was a small murmur among the press benches. Why was a witness requiring legal representation?

Following the two marathon interviews with Inspector Narborough, Stillwell and his family realised that he was in serious trouble. His uncle, his mother's brother, recommended that he see Vincent Jackson, a solicitor he had some experience or knowledge of, based in Arundel. Mr Jackson immediately advised his client not to speak to the police again without his presence.

Nicole Ashby, Joan's friend from the YWCA, was the first person to step into the witness-box. She recounted the last time she saw Joan on the morning of 31 July and how Joan had said she was going home for the weekend; she detailed the clothes Joan had been wearing and the luggage she had been carrying. Poignantly, Nicole confirmed that the next time she had seen any of those clothes and items was when shown them by Arundel police. Mr Falconer for the family asked the girl to confirm that Joan was a girl of exemplary moral character. Nicole replied firmly, 'Yes.'

Ida Sheriff took the stand next. She was nervous, and her hands trembled. She explained how Joan knew Box Copse and how she liked sun-bathing and how she would sometimes shed her dress to do this. A suppressed gasp in the courtroom at this statement unsettled her, and she quickly moved on to say that her niece was of excellent character.

'Her way of life was beyond question, altogether,' she stressed.

She was asked to explain why Joan would not have had her dressing-gown in her case, and Ida was assured in her reply. 'I think that in the first place she intended to come home, and in that case she would not have needed her dressing-gown at all, and when she found herself among the crowds she came down to Arundel.'

Mr Falconer probed Ida further if only to amplify the great distress that had been caused by the slurs on Joan's character and how utterly off-target the family believed they were. They were determined to use this public forum to redress the wrongs they felt had been wrought upon Joan's name. Stillwell's solicitor, Mr Jackson, asked Ida to confirm that her niece would only sunbathe where she would expect privacy. Mrs Sheriff agreed.

Dr John Gordon Hunt, the local pathologist who had assisted Dr Keith

Simpson at the scene and in the mortuary, followed in the witness-box. He said that although there was decomposition of the head otherwise the body was well preserved. He estimated she was a woman of about thirty years of age. He said she had definitely been strangled. He also confirmed that there had been forcible sexual interference.

Mr Jackson, for Stillwell, was up on his feet to cross-examine. He attempted to get the doctor to concede that because he had estimated that the body had been there between seven and ten days then Joan could have been killed as late as Tuesday 3 August. Mr Porter objected to the line of questioning, pointing to the evidence of Joan's deposit of her suitcase at Worthing Station at midday on Saturday 31 July.

Mr Butler, the coroner, seemed a little confused. 'We are merely making an inquiry into this in order to record a death,' he said. Mr Jackson's pre-emptive strike served only to convince independent observers that Stillwell needed defending, but nobody yet knew why.

Fifty-one minutes into the inquest Thomas Stillwell took the stand. Mr Butler fixed his eye on him and said, 'I have to caution you that you are not bound to answer any questions that might incriminate you, but whatever you do say will taken down in writing and may be used in evidence on some other occasion. Do you follow?'

'Yes.'

Mr Jackson rose to his feet. 'I appear on behalf of this witness. I wish to say he has already made statements and given evidence at the first inquest. Already given evidence, sir, and that evidence could be repeated, but if our friends are wishing to deal with those statements which he has subsequently made, before any of these are made public in any way, I should want to make a submission that they are not admissible, but apart from that we are here to assist the court to the best of our ability.'

The coroner agreed. Therefore none of the new circumstantial evidence that emanated from Stillwell's later statements could be aired in court. To a layman this might be understandable if a criminal trial were known to be following. But was it?

Mr Butler began to question Stillwell himself.

'Do you remember giving evidence before me on 13 August? Did you say on that occasion that during the afternoon of Tuesday 10 August, about a quarter to five, you were taking a short cut through park to your home?'

'I did.'

'Is that a fact?'

'It is, and it isn't.'

Confused expectancy spread across faces across the courtroom.

'That you were taking a short cut through the park?'

'I was going through the park.'

Having isolated the short-cut anomaly the coroner moved on, encouraging Stillwell to recount his discovery of the body and how the corpse was clothed. Stillwell said he never touched the body. The elderly man then addressed the day of the murder.

'Were you in Arundel Park on the Saturday before the bank holiday, 31 July?'

'I don't remember, to be accurate.'

'Do you mean you cannot remember the date?'

'I can't remember being there on that date.'

Those in the room familiar with Stillwell's police statements would have noted a significant shift away from what he had said earlier.

'On some previous occasion did you see a lady in the park? Did you speak to a woman?'

'Yes.'

'And did she answer you?'

'No.'

'Was she anywhere near Box Copse where the body was found?'

'Near the walnut tree, which is down the bottom.'

'Do you mean in Box Copse?'

'No.'

'What was she doing?'

'Just walking.'

'In which direction?'

'When I spoke to her she was walking back round towards the lake.'

'Towards the lake, you say? Would that take her past Box Copse?'

'Yes, the path runs along the bottom of Box Copse.'

'Did you follow her?'

'No, not after. I didn't follow her round the lake.'

'Did you follow her with your eyes? Could you see where she was going?'

'I followed her round towards the lake. Yes.'

'Did you notice how she was dressed?'

'This woman had on a brown swagger coat, actually. I should say it was a swagger.' (A swagger coat was a three-quarter-length woman's coat that flared out loosely from the shoulders; it first appeared during the 1930s.)

Those disbelieving of Stillwell would have thought that he had introduced the brown swagger coat (and his new vagueness about the precise day) into his evidence to move the lady in his police statements away from the likelihood of it being Joan Woodhouse. Unfortunately, the coroner did not ask the witness about the weather, as it would have been highly incongruous for anybody to be wearing a coat of any sort on the hottest day of the year.

Mr Porter, the solicitor for the police, stood to cross-examine, determined to find a route into Stillwell's conflicting statements and highlight them.

'When you originally reported this matter, the finding of the body to the police, did you say you were taking a short cut through Box Copse?'

'Yes.'

'Was that in fact the case?'

'I was, but I wasn't.'

'Were you taking a short cut, or were you not?'

'It would have been a short cut, yes.'

'Tell me. Some months ago did you suffer an injury to your leg?'

'Quite correct.'

'And does that injury make it difficult for you to tackle hilly ground?'

'Slightly.'

'Would it make it difficult for you to tackle the ground which you say you were using as a short cut?'

'My foot would hurt, but I would make it.'

'Did you subsequently tell the police that you were not taking a short cut through Box Copse?'

'I agree it was a difficult passage.'

'I asked you if you subsequently told the police you were not taking a short cut?'

The solicitor's voice rose as his impatience with Stillwell's evasiveness built.

Mr Jackson rose to his feet before his client could reply.

'Sir, I think we had better get this cleared up with your permission, now.

My friend is quite obviously attempting to cross-examine on the confidential statements which were made by this man, Stillwell, to the police. I have already intimated in my submission that they are not admissible in evidence owing to the circumstances in which they were taken, and if my friend is persisting in this line of cross-examination I must take up the time of the court by making my submission. He cannot continue.'

What were the circumstances in which the police statements were taken that made them inadmissible in evidence? And would this apply at any potential criminal trial? Inspector Narborough does not enlighten us in his detailed account of this hearing. Was Mr Jackson objecting to the length of time Stillwell was questioned for in that two-day session? Or was there an issue over mistreatment – sleep deprivation, perhaps?

A legal spat developed between Messrs Porter and Jackson over what could and could not be asked of the witness. The coroner then took up the questioning once more. He asked Stillwell to look at a photograph of Joan Woodhouse, and he seemed reluctant to do so, saying he had seen it many times before. He said he was certain it was *not* the woman he spoke to.

Mr Porter reverted to the short-cut conundrum but still could not penetrate Stillwell's armoury and finally agreed to leave that line of questioning. He went on to Stillwell's statement to the police that he had been in the park on 31 July. The witness said the police said witnesses had seen him in the park on that day so he agreed he must have been. He remembered saying good morning to the girl he had seen and that she ignored him but made no mention of the 'Bugger you, then' he had told the police he had said. He was insistent that the girl he had encountered was not Joan Woodhouse. He ended his evidence by telling the court how he had borrowed a bike from the lodge by Swanbourne Lake, where he was known, and cycled to the police station after he had found the body on August 10.

Nobody asked why he did not ask the lodge keeper to use his telephone rather than choose to ride around a mile to the police station.

Something had been troubling the jury, and at this point the foreman asked if he could speak.

'The jury would like to know if it is normal, or if there are any special reasons why this witness should be legally represented if he is only giving evidence about finding the body?'

'I am not only giving evidence about finding the body,' Stillwell interjected.

'The question the jury is asking is, is there any particular significance in his being legally represented?' continued the foreman, addressing Mr Butler and ignoring Stillwell.

'I cannot tell you. You must use your own judgement about that.'

Inspector Narborough was the final witness called. He took the jury through his first days on the case and talked of the murder scene and commented that the body was facially unrecognisable and how he now concluded that Joan had been murdered by a complete stranger. He ended his prepared statement by saying that up to now the police were unable to produce sufficient evidence to enable them to institute criminal proceedings.

In answer to a question from the jury Narborough said he believed that Joan had been lying on the folded clothing when she was attacked and that she struggled there, hence the kick marks on the tree, and ran down the pathway to where her body was found and where her murderer had actually caught up with her.

Mr Falconer for the family pressed the policeman on his views of Joan's character and whether any evidence of any secret lover had been discovered, bearing in mind the speculation in national newspapers. Narborough confirmed he believed Joan to be of excellent character and he was certain there was no secret lover but stopped short of criticising the press coverage. Indeed, he went on to take the opportunity to thank the newspapers for the publicity they had given the case and which was helping the police in their efforts to solve the crime.

Mr Butler finally asked the policeman to confirm that the investigation was still ongoing.

'It is still under observation and by no means closed,' was Narborough's response, one that would not have inspired the family.

Sixty-five years later, in 2013, Fred Narborough's daughter can remember her father coming home and being very frustrated by the hearing. He commented on the great age of the coroner and thought his grasp of the case was poor and claimed that at times he even mixed up names of witnesses and other details. Fred felt that had Mr Butler permitted an airing of Stillwell's near confession and his own admission of the sexual motives of his park visit the case would have taken a very different path.

After giving some guidance, Mr Butler retired the jury to reach their verdict. They were back inside five minutes. Joan Woodhouse, they announced, was murdered by some person or persons unknown.

9
ON THE STREETS OF ARUNDEL

If Inspector Narborough and anyone else was hoping that the Woodhouse family would, now the inquest was complete, relax their scrutiny of him and the investigation they were very much mistaken. For Narborough to stand up in court and say the case merely remained under observation was alarming. Surely the murderer was in their sights and they needed to do more than observe?

The Woodhouse family's faith in Scotland Yard and their will to solve the murder of their loved one was diminishing by the day. Even then the public was familiar with police-speak: Narborough's 'still under observation and by no means closed' was not far short of the 'we are not looking for anyone else in connection with this crime' that the police make use of when they have failed to secure a guilty verdict but want the public to know that as far as they are concerned they had the right person.

Mr Woodhouse and his sisters-in-law hoped, though, that they were turning the tide of the newspaper innuendo about Joan's character and implied love life. Narborough had been made to say publicly at the inquest that Joan was of exemplary character and that reports of a secret life were completely wrong. This was an implicit admission by the policeman of how the investigation had been misguided. Through their solicitor in Hull, a Mr Arnold Dickinson, the family were successful in taking the *Sunday Pictorial* to task. The *Pictorial*, a forerunner of the *Sunday Mirror* and owned by the Harmsworth family, had, in the family's opinion, been particularly lurid and misleading, and Dickinson managed to persuade them under threat of legal action to print an apology and even publish Joan's Rule of Life to banish any doubt. This they duly did.

As Christmas 1948 approached the Woodhouse family could sense the trail becoming as cold as the severe winter that was disrupting the country.

They held a conference and, for the first time, decided that Narborough was not up to the task, that his heart was not in it. His mind elsewhere. Tied to his own failure and therefore unable to innovate. They felt they would, in Ida's words, have to 'get on his case'. They took turns to write letters to him, pressing him on progress. Asking for updates. What had he done about this and what about that? Gathering up the loose ends and laying them down in front of him. They suspected that he was embarrassed, or worse, about his failings in the investigation. A high-profile court case could ruin his career, as his pursuing the secret-lover tangent and the subsequent loss of potential forensic and material evidence would be broadcast nationally. Perhaps he believed that a jury could not convict Stillwell on circumstantial evidence alone and therefore the country would blame him for allowing a murderer of a good, English girl to walk free. The family were rapidly moving towards the view that Narborough was frightened that if Stillwell went on trial, so would he.

On 7 January 1949 Mr Woodhouse and the two aunts got in front of Inspector Narborough again at Scotland Yard at 4 Whitehall Place, London. They interrogated *him*. He already knew the sisters; despite looking like the little old ladies one might see clutching their handbags on their laps sitting passively in bus shelters, they were dogged and determined, but today he could see that they were also formidable, steely. His heart must have sunk. In his autobiography he rues: 'I never guessed how the determination of these two frail elderly women was to affect my future even after I had left the Metropolitan Police.'

He still had little to placate them with. He estimated that if he charged Thomas Stillwell there was only a 60 per cent chance that a jury would convict. And? Why were they not good enough odds, wondered the family? He also revealed that he had been to see Mr Jackson, Stillwell's solicitor, and suggested that his client might like to say the murder of Joan was an accident and then the Crown would only pursue a manslaughter charge. Jackson refused point-blank. His client was completely innocent, he retorted. Lena Bamber recalls that this admission shocked the Woodhouse family to the core. Under what authority had the policeman acted in this way? How dare he go off making potential plea deals without consulting them.

Narborough reiterated that he still felt the best chance of being able to lay charges at Stillwell's door was if the suspect, himself, slipped up. He pointed out that Stillwell had broken down once in interview so was not impervious to pressure. Astonishingly, he suggested that the family should visit Arundel regularly and be seen about town. Let Stillwell know they were there. That he had not got away with murder. Make him uneasy and put him on edge. Perhaps he will crack, said Narborough. John Woodhouse thought he could hear a barrel being scraped and did not think he could control himself to confront Stillwell in any way, but the aunts readily agreed to giving this irregular strategy a try.

Sometimes it was just Ida and Annie who went, but on other occasions Lena Bamber and other sisters and friends of Joan's late mother would accompany them. They stayed in the Norfolk Hotel and other places in the main square in Arundel and became well known in the tea rooms and shops or just walking around the old town. They visited the spot where Joan died and built a little shrine, carving Joan's initials into the bark of the tree in Box Copse by which her clothes had been folded and piled. They were touched, heartened and encouraged by the welcome they received from the townspeople. Some expressed horror and sorrow that such a violent act could have taken place in their lovely little community.

Others wished them luck saying, 'We all know who done it.'

Lena claimed to the author that people named Stillwell to them frequently, adding that he was a menace to all the town's women. The sisters urged these people to go to the police and repeat what they said there, but they shook their heads and just said, 'They knows.'

Not one person on any of their visits spoke in defence of the suspect, according to the family. Nobody told them to go away. To move on. If this man was indeed innocent it was extraordinary harassment of a suspect suggested, sanctioned and encouraged by Scotland Yard.

Ida and Annie discovered that Thomas Stillwell was courting and planned to become engaged to and marry a local girl. She was younger than him, and Stillwell had met her when delivering meat to her house years before. She had been sickly as a child, and Stillwell, and later his mother, had assisted her in nursing her ailing father, a retired gamekeeper. The sisters found out that Tom's fiancée worked in a millinery shop and bowled in there and pleaded with her to see sense, to denounce her intended as a murderer. The poor young girl's reaction to such a tense situation is not known but can be guessed.

On one occasion an older sister of Ida, Annie and Joan's dead mother was in town, too. She was Molly, and by all accounts more strident even than Ida. This day there was Ida, Annie, Lena Bamber and Molly. Lena recalled in 2010:

> Somebody told us where Stillwell was working. He was painting a newly-built house on the outskirts of the town centre. We walked there and waited, knowing he would finish soon. It was around tea-time. When he came out and saw us he was startled but put his head down and wheeled his bike towards us as we were by the gate. Aunt Molly stepped forward. I think she put her hand on the handlebars stopping him.
>
> 'Have you got anything to say for yourself?' she boomed.
>
> Stillwell was still looking at the ground. He would not look up. I could see his hands were shaking. He was trembling like a leaf and as white as a sheet.
>
> 'Well?' Molly said.
>
> It was all over in seconds, I expect, but it felt like an age. I really thought he was going to say something. He did not protest his innocence. He did not turn nasty. I could see he was swallowing hard and breathing heavily, and I think he wanted to unburden himself, but then he turned the front wheel to the side, jumped on the saddle and pedalled off furiously.

This campaign of confrontation conducted by the elderly women did not, however, yield any results, and finally, to the horror of the family, in March 1949 Inspector Fred Narborough announced he was abandoning the investigation. He knew he had failed miserably.

In his autobiography he makes the following comment:

> I read the newspapers like the rest. I knew, with a curse on my lips, that the murderer was mouthing over the same headlines in his secret place, with a grin on his face.
>
> Small things constantly remind me of the investigation which failed ten years ago. A pause at the traffic lights, a sideways glance to a shop window where there is the assistant in stockinged feet draping underwear across headless dummies of young women. In the countryside, a rabbit thumping towards the safety of the burrow, away from the noise of my car. Even bees bumbling their way among the flowers in my garden at home.
>
> All the time, there is that murder on my mind.

And that is the passage with which Inspector Narborough ends his book – 'murder on my mind'. Although the heavy hand of a ghost-writer appears to be evident, Joan's tragic case dominates the whole work and at times it reads like an open apology letter to her memory and the Woodhouse family.

Mr Woodhouse and the aunts protested vociferously about the case being closed but to no avail. Now they understood they were going to have to go over Narborough's head to a higher authority. In the end this was decided for them, for when they tried to seek further audience with him they were shocked to be told that the 46-year-old policeman had 'retired'. Narborough himself would have disagreed with the retirement explanation, and a small diary piece in *The Straits Times* of 25 September 1949 suggests other reasons for his departure:

> Many of Scotland Yard's top detectives are deeply dissatisfied with their pay, despite increases just granted on the recommendation of the Oaksey Committee.
>
> Now comes the news that Superintendent Fred Narborough is resigning his £800-a-year job as a member of the murder squad. He is 46; he may take a job with the Allied Control Commission in Germany; was there recently investigating a murder.
>
> This is the third resignation in a few weeks at the Yard.

Whatever the truth, the fact remains that Fred Narborough's Scotland Yard career only survived a few months after the abandonment of the Joan Woodhouse murder investigation.

10
ENTER JACKS

Joan's father felt deserted, abandoned and let down by Scotland Yard and wrote to the home secretary, the public prosecutor and the attorney general hoping they would see sense and instruct the police to reopen the case immediately. On 24 April 1949 his letter made the following points:

Why were people who lived on the Duke of Norfolk's Arundel estate where Joan's body was found not questioned in the immediate aftermath of the murder? Instead police searched for a male companion even when witnesses stated they saw a girl fitting Joan's description in Arundel – alone.

Why was Thomas Stillwell's bandaged hand – that was on display at the adjourned inquest – not investigated? He may well have been playing it up so he could say he could not have strangled Joan, but then one would put the question how was he then going to catch the rabbits he claimed he was in Box Copse looking for? Alternatively, could his hand have been bitten by Joan? We will never know because by the time he was questioned the hand had healed.

There was a struggle evidenced by the marks on the bark of the tree in Box Copse. Equally suspect's boots would have shown marks. Why was this not followed up?

Suspect has admitted seeing Joan at Box Copse 'probably on July 31'. She was not there on any other day so he has placed himself at the scene of the crime.

Who was briefing the press with erroneous information that encouraged them to go off and write scurrilous, misleading and slanderous information about Joan?

Why was Stillwell's statement about a 'short cut' first taken at face value? Box Copse is a short cut to nowhere!

Stillwell said he dropped the dart found at the scene when he discovered the body. How did that just drop out his pocket if there was no struggle? If he just stumbled on the body and walked by it? Did it fall out on the day she was murdered?

In the letter to Hartley Shawcross, the attorney general and a Labour MP, Mr Woodhouse says the family had been 'deprived of justice' and refers to their 'deep conviction that because of the flaws in the investigation' the situation had come about. He finishes off with an appeal: 'Would you be good enough, at your convenience, to make an appointment for Mrs Sheriff and myself to see you, please.'

They didn't get their meeting, instead receiving sympathetic but immovable replies. These higher powers were not going to be easily persuaded to question a senior, respected Scotland Yard inspector's competence and, anyhow, he had now left. Narborough had retired from his £800-a-year post (about £65,000 at current values) and was now working in the commercial sector in Germany. The family were told verbally, Lena Bamber insisted in 2010, that Narborough had been eased out and that the Yard indicated that they, the family, should take some comfort from that.

There is, and remains, a long culture in the English police forces of officers being 'retired' or written off sick when complaints are made against them or allegations of any sort that are difficult to rebut. Also, throughout the public sector in the UK there is a school of thought that somebody losing their post should be sufficient to assuage external dissatisfaction.

This stonewalling left the Woodhouse family devastated. Not only were they attempting to deal with the grief of losing Joan in such horrendous and violent circumstances but they also had to bear the attacks on her character and now the denial of justice.

On top of this, her memory had now been dragged into a sordid netherworld. In July a man called Sidney Chamberlain was hanged for the murder of his girlfriend Doreen Messenger. Another prisoner claimed that just before his execution Chamberlain had confessed to the murder of Joan. It was patently untrue, but it created sensational headlines for a couple of days. There were others, too. Joan Woodhouse became *the* unsolved murder that assorted crackpots felt the need to confess to.

Joan's former home in Park Road, Barnsley, was a sombre place as her father struggled painfully with his very worst nightmare. Meanwhile, over in Bridlington Ida Sheriff and Annie Blades refused to be beaten into submission by faceless civil servants. If the police or the legal system would not seek justice for Joan then *they* would. Apart from anything else it was their Christian duty.

They launched a fund for a private inquiry and floated it with £500 of their own money. After some press publicity a Herbert Bland of Tachbrook Street, London SW1, weighed in with £105 of his own money. He had no connection to the family but said he had followed the case and thought it intolerable that the inquiry had been closed.

The aunts also put up a reward for information leading to the arrest of Joan's killer and revealed to the newspapers that anything they would spend on their quest was money that would have been left to Joan on their deaths in any case.

In a letter in the family collection Ida disclosed that she had tried to offer a reward earlier, but Inspector Narborough had persuaded her that it could be counter-productive.

'We all know Stillwell did it,' she says she was told by the policeman. 'If you put up a reward it might encourage people to perjure themselves, and then we could lose the whole case.'

She could see the logic in his argument then when there was all to play for, and she believed the net was closing in on Stillwell, but now the playing field had changed.

The two elderly ladies also asked their solicitor to recommend a good private detective and he immediately thought of the man who had carried out so much 'divorce work' for him. His name was Thomas Percy Jacks.

Ironically, Thomas Jacks had a very similar background and upbringing to Inspector Narborough, the man he was, in a sense, replacing. He was born in 1897 in Burnham, Norfolk, to Job and Mary Jacks, and when his father secured the position as gamekeeper on the Queen's nearby Sandringham Estate they moved across the county to the village of Houghton.

Here he learned his father's trade and skills, and when he left school at the age of fifteen in 1912 he took a job as an underkeeper on the Sunderlandwick estate in Driffield, Yorkshire. The First World War interrupted Thomas' apprenticeship, and he, saying he was nineteen when he was in fact seventeen, joined the Royal Field Artillery and saw action in France.

After surviving the war he returned to Driffield, but he wanted more from his life than gamekeeping, and in 1919 he joined the East Riding County Constabulary as a young policeman. Shortly after that he married Maud Railton, and four sons and one daughter followed. Meanwhile, with quiet ambition, he progressed through the ranks, rising to the rank of detective sergeant, although during the Second World War he became an acting inspector and was bitterly disappointed when another man got the next vacant inspector post ahead of him when peace was restored. When he was able to take retirement and his pension after twenty-five years in the force, he did so. He exchanged his £8 10s a week wage for a £182-a-year pension. He later told the *Daily Mirror* that during his career as a policeman he had appeared in the witness-box 3,000 times and had made 500 successful prosecutions but acknowledged that the Joan Woodhouse case was only the second murder he had worked on.

From the Yorkshire force he went to Germany, taking a post as a detective in the military police and stayed in mainland Europe for a couple of years. Unfortunately, his marriage to Maud did not survive this overseas posting. On his return he decided to take further control of his own destiny and set up as a private detective, working at first from offices on the promenade at Bridlington. He had business cards printed up – Jacks' Detective Agency – and waited for the work to roll in. He was by now living with another woman, and she would help in her partner's business, although she principally ran the gown shop next door. The shop specialised in dresses for larger women.

A newspaper profile of Jacks after the Arundel case had made him temporarily famous described him as being fifteen stone, wearing a grey-green suit of Lovat tweed and size eight brown shoes. He smoked an ounce of pipe tobacco a day.

Setting up as a sleuth was a familiar route taken by senior ex-policemen who were not prepared (or able) to live off their pensions and tend their roses when still only in their forties. Public perception of private detectives ranged from Sherlock Holmes in Britain to the shadowy Sam Spade, personified by Humphrey Bogart in Hollywood movies, but the reality was somewhat different. Like Thomas Jacks, they were often nondescript, responsible, upstanding citizens who worked closely with solicitors in tracing missing persons, investigating company and insurance fraud and advising people on security issues. Much work was done over the telephone and at the desk, although divorce cases sometimes entailed covert surveillance and photography to prove adultery.

Divorce is now a much easier and common process, but in the mid-twentieth century a client would have to have solid grounds (and proof) for a court to grant this final legal separation. Jacks told his son Ronald that he was manhandled a few times in the course of these investigations.

Ronald, who was in his early twenties when his father became a private detective, remembered his father in 2010:

> He was a strict father and was not shy about giving us a clip around the ear when we were kids. Mind you, that were common then, and it was probably no bad thing. As a policeman he had a reputation as a hard man. He'd pinch his own grandmother if she broke the law, they said of him. Having said that he was a sociable man and everyone knew him in Bridlington. He liked to visit the pubs and could mix with all sorts. I think the business gave him a reasonable lifestyle, and he was certainly a member of one of those organisations – freemasons or one of them. Him and Lou (his second wife) were well suited and seemed happy.

Jacks would not have been in business long when his contact, the solicitor Arnold Dickinson, told him he had a potentially very interesting case and sent him along to Albion Terrace to meet Ida Sheriff and Annie Blades. The two ladies were presented with a well-dressed, 52-year-old, plump and red-cheeked man when they took tea with him that afternoon in September 1949. He was confident and avuncular. He listened to their story. As an ex-policeman he would have been aware of the case but would not have known the finer details. He revealed his charges to them – two guineas a day – and then said he would be delighted to take it on.

On Monday 10 October 1949, having cleared his desk and tied up all his outstanding work, Thomas Jacks arrived in Arundel and settled into the 10s 6d-a-night guesthouse he had booked. He would end up staying for several weeks.

11

A COMPELLING DOSSIER

First thing the following Tuesday morning Thomas Jacks presented himself at Arundel Police Station. As a recently retired policeman himself he was very aware of the required etiquette and the importance of not alienating the local force – and, of course, Scotland Yard, although he felt the latter might be difficult.

Sergeant Bristow welcomed him warmly and took him personally to Box Copse and went over the details of the day that Stillwell took them to see the body. Jacks is adamant in his papers that Sergeant Bristow told him that the Arundel police believed Stillwell to be guilty – as did most townspeople – although he concedes the sergeant later changed his public stance. Jacks was surprised but secretly excited that Bristow also handed over an inquiry file on the case that he really should not have and hurriedly went back to his hotel room and transcribed laboriously on a typewriter Stillwell's full police statements before promptly returning the originals.

Police archive files show that Scotland Yard and West Sussex police bosses were horrified that Sergeant Bristow had taken Jacks into his confidence and had co-operated with him so openly and keenly. The contents of those Stillwell statements had never been aired outside of the four walls of a police station or a solicitor's office, and they knew that if they ever were the public demand to charge the suspect would be overwhelming. For whatever reason, they did not want to follow that path.

A flurry of typed memos circulated between the forces, and various senior officers, and the sacking of Sergeant Bristow was discussed. Eventually it was decided that sacking Bristow would be counter-productive, and one memo cites the reason that it would encourage media scrutiny of the investigation of the case, 'which would not be welcome' according to a memorandum stored in police files at the West Sussex Record Office. Why would media scrutiny not be welcome? Unfortunately the police files do not enlighten us.

Bristow took early retirement, according to police files housed in Chichester Library. This appears to be proof, if any is needed, that Scotland Yard and West Sussex Police were extremely sensitive about the investigation of the case, and there were aspects that they feared would not stand up to the media spotlight. It certainly adds weight to the family's belief that Stillwell was not charged to save police embarrassment.

Those statements, however, convinced the private detective of Stillwell's culpability and supported everything the aunts had told him about police evasiveness. Professionally, he was amazed that Inspector Narborough felt there was not enough evidence here to at least lay charges and put it in front a jury to allow them to decide – during his career he had seen far weaker cases prosecuted. His gut feeling already was that Narborough did not want the light of truth beaming into his investigation, just as the aunts had suggested. However, he would conduct his investigation with discipline, rigour and an open mind. He was confident that by the end of it his dossier would be so compelling that Scotland Yard, or any other body, would ignore it at their peril.

On Friday his promising start was impeded by a tense meeting with the Chief Constable of West Sussex Police, Detective Superintendent Eagle. The chief constable informed the private detective in no uncertain terms that he would get no co-operation from them whatsoever.

'Just because the family of the deceased are dissatisfied, do you really expect us to reopen the case?' Jacks recalls Eagle barking.

Even though Eagle was highly disapproving of the private detective's intervention he asked that anything he did find out be passed on to him in Chichester and not to the police locally in Arundel. Jacks thought this a bit rich. However, he agreed but soon realised that even though he quickly began to pass leads on the police were not acting on them. Jacks rapidly reached the opinion that something stank. At the lower levels the police wanted a conviction and encouraged him, but higher up he was being frustrated at every turn.

There was no shortage of people from Arundel who would tell him that Stillwell was his man, but the detective needed proof not opinion or gossip. The locals seemed to open up to him more than they would to the police.

However, eventually, as he methodically worked through every lead and interviewed scores of potential witnesses, he amassed some credible evidence. One of these witnesses was Frederick George Chamberlain, publican of the Black Rabbit.

Chamberlain had encountered Stillwell on the late afternoon of 10 August 1948. This was the day Stillwell reported finding the body to the police. If Chamberlain is correct in his recollection he was coming out of the post office, and Stillwell stopped on a bike and spoke to him. The two men were very familiar with one another, Stillwell being a regular in Chamberlain's pub and a member of the darts team.

Chamberlain's statement describes the encounter as follows:

'What's happened to you, Tom?' Chamberlain said pointing to Stillwell's bandaged hand.

'This is the least of my worries,' replied Stillwell. 'I've just found a body.'

'A body! What, an old person?' asked Chamberlain, thinking someone of senior years may have become disorientated in the park and collapsed as they sometimes did.

'No, a young girl of about twenty-six or twenty-seven.'

'Blimey! Well, you best go and report it then.'

'I am. That's where I'm off.'

At first Jacks believed that the key significance of this witness statement was that it contradicted Stillwell's breathless, excitable manner witnessed by Bristow and others when he entered the police station. Would someone who had genuinely been rushing to report the finding of a body stop to pass the time of a day with an acquaintance? But soon something even more significant would emerge from this recollection that the private detective believed incriminated the suspect in a crucial way.

Among other witnesses located by Jacks were local men Phil Challen and Frank Clements, who believed they saw Thomas Stillwell in Arundel Park on the Saturday, the estimated day of the murder, and remember speaking with him and then observed him walking uphill to Box Copse. Therefore there were now new, reliable witnesses who placed Stillwell at the scene of the murder and at the correct time. Jacks supported these statements with other people, including André Buller, the boatman on Swanbourne Lake, who also saw and conversed with the suspect on that Saturday, 31 July.

It beggars belief that Narborough's investigation did not uncover these witnesses. As soon as Stillwell came under suspicion, would it not make sense to interview the people who had seen him on the day he allegedly discovered the body? Wouldn't the police want to know about his demeanour on the day he found a corpse? Wouldn't they want to know what he had told the people he played darts with about his day? As someone who saw him regularly, would they not have wanted to chat in detail with the landlord of his local pub?

Regularly reporting back to Joan's aunts and father, Jacks was growing more confident by the day that whatever 'political' problems there were with the case the cumulative power of his evidence would be irresistible. During November, though, some six weeks into his inquiry, Thomas Jacks had *his* moment of absolute clarity.

He had previously been shown harrowing police photographs of Joan Woodhouse's body and the murder scene. Close-ups of her head showed that the several days in intense heat and being open to the elements and foraging wild-life had rendered her features unrecognisable. It was the private detective's firm opinion that no person could say with any confidence that this was the body of a woman in her twenties, thirties, forties or fifties. His mind clicked back to his conversation with the Black Rabbit licensee, George Chamberlain. He had remembered Stillwell saying he had discovered a woman's body. A woman he said was not old and had added that she was about twenty-six or twenty-seven years old. If he had not met that woman before or had no knowledge of the body, how could he have possibly known so accurately how old she was? In Jacks' opinion Stillwell, whom he now regarded as a very cunning individual, had slipped up.

Another significant witness unearthed by Jacks was a John Mobey. The private detective felt he was potentially as significant as George Chamberlain. Mobey recalled bumping into Stillwell, who was an acquaintance but not a friend, on Arundel Bridge. It was the day of the inquest, and Stillwell told Mobey where he had been and began to talk about the murder. Mobey felt it was strange that they were having the conversation and even more bizarre when Stillwell volunteered the information that 'he always went to the pictures on Saturdays'. Mobey's curiosity was piqued further when he met Stillwell again at the café at the local cinema a couple of Saturdays later and joined him at his table to drink tea. Mobey remembers it well because Stillwell tossed a coin to see who would pay for the tea and lost. Mobey thought the encounters strange, but Jacks detected a clumsy attempt to create an alibi.

After interviewing more than 200 people, following up countless leads and checking and rechecking hundreds of facts and previous statements, Thomas Jacks sat down in early December 1949 and typed up his final dossier to present to his client and to Scotland Yard. He had been on the job fifty-five days, and his bill to Ida Sheriff and Annie Blades would come to 110 guineas plus expenses. Their quest for justice would today cost an amount equivalent to more than £4,000, not counting the £500 reward still on offer.

Thomas Jacks was comfortable that he had given his clients value for their money. He had no doubt that he had laid down the vital plank for the Woodhouse family to use in their final quest for justice. Unpalatable as it might be, Scotland Yard would have to acknowledge he was a former police detective himself with an impeccable record and would have to respect the work he had done and act upon it. He was sure that within months a jury would be deciding whether or not Thomas Stillwell of Foxes' Oven, Offham, would be meeting the executioner.

'I will never give up this case,' he declared. 'A murderer has already destroyed one sweet, God-fearing girl, and he may strike again. My duty ends the day a man is charged. It is for the court to decide his guilt.'

Stillwell, on the other hand, must have been feeling confident his ordeal was over having seen the police investigation peter out and thinking that Jacks' private investigation had gone nowhere. He detailed his relief and personal trials in the story he sold to the *Sunday Pictorial* on 26 February 1950.

WHISPERS ARE RUINING THE LIVES OF TWO YOUNG PEOPLE

For a start get this straight. I never knew Joan Woodhouse, the girl who was murdered in Arundel Park 18 months ago. My only connection with the tragedy was that I found the body.

It is difficult to recall when I first became aware that malicious stories were being told about me behind my back. When it started, you could hardly call it gossip. It was more like leg-pulling. But gradually a whisper here and there grew into something more.

One woman said to another woman that I must have done the murder, and the tales came back to me with such cracks as 'Have you found any more bodies yet, Tommy?'

My family worried about it far more than I did. My mother was on the verge of a nervous breakdown. And every one of us felt that wherever we went we were being pointed out.

That has been going on for 18 months. Sometimes people say to me: 'Why don't you go away and make a fresh start somewhere else?'

But why should I? I've done nothing wrong. I was born in Arundel, and it is my home.

There has never been anything 'secretive' about the way I live.

I am, for instance, a keen footballer. I used to play for Arundel, but for some reason I didn't get a game, so I transferred to Rustington.

And, although I don't drink, I am also a keen darts player. I used to play for the Newburgh Arms team. I don't belong to that or any other team any longer because this sort of social contact has become embarrassing since people began talking.

What has encouraged me more than anything else is the love and confidence of the girl who has promised to marry me. She was a playmate of mine when we were children – became engaged to me last June.

And although she has complete faith in me, and is ready to marry me tomorrow, I want to clear the air of all of these horrible suspicions before she becomes my wife.

Somehow this mystery has got to be solved. That would be the very best wedding present anyone could give us.

How I found the body of Joan Woodhouse happened this way: Just before five o'clock on the afternoon of August 10, 1948, I was walking through the wood known locally as Box Copse, near the edge of Swanbourne Lake and about a mile from Arundel Castle.

Pile of clothes

Two little girls, whom I did not recognise, were playing near the edge of the wood when I reached it. Under the trees the bright colours of a little pile of clothing caught my eye.

At first I thought it was a head scarf, but when I picked it up I saw that it was a Paisley dress. There was also a light summer coat – fawn, I think – and a green waterproof.

There was also a knitting bag, which I picked up and opened with the idea of trying to identify the owner. But the contents were soaking wet – evidently it had been out in the rain – so I took out only a pair of sunglasses, which I put in my breast pocket.

Then I caught sight of the body. It was lying about 30ft. away, below me on sloping ground. My first thought was that someone had been injured and I believe I called out, though I can't be sure. Moving closer, I saw that it was the body of a girl, naked except for what I took to be a vest. Later I was told that what she had on was camiknickers. She also had stockings and sandals.

The girl was lying on her back and the sight of her face was a great shock to me.

I was a bit shaken, but I remembered to put the sunglasses back in the knitting bag, and in bending down to do this I must have dropped a brass dart which had been in my pocket and was subsequently found by the police.

I did not want to alarm the children by telling them about the body, so I warned them not to go into the wood with some story about cattle which might frighten them.

Then I hurried down to the Lake Lodge to report what I had found. The first person I met was my mother walking home with her shopping. I told her I was going to the police.

At the police station the constable on duty thought I was pulling his leg when I said there was a girl's body in the park. He knew me, of course – everybody knows everybody in a little place like Arundel. But when he realised I was serious, the police went into action at once.

The first indication I had that the police suspected that I might have had something to do with the murder was when I was called to the police station and questioned for four hours.

At nine-thirty on the following morning a police car came to fetch me from the place where I was working and the questioning was resumed – this time for ten hours.

All night

They were quite nice to me, of course, and gave me dinner and took me home in their car. The next day I was asked to go to the police station again on my way home from work, and this time they kept me all night. Scotland Yard officers were there, and they went over my story again and again. I signed the statement I had made the previous day, although I was too weary to read it all.

At the adjourned inquest the verdict was murder by some person or persons unknown, I thought that was the end of it all, and that my name had been cleared.

BUT I RECKONED WITHOUT THE GOSSIPMONGERS. IN FACT, MY ORDEAL WAS ONLY BEGINNING.

Reading this now, and knowing what Stillwell had told the police about what he did or wanted to do to the two little girls he saw after allegedly finding the body, whether he was guilty or not, one can only conclude that the suspect was either stupid or incredibly arrogant. He also mentions for the first time taking Joan's sunglasses out of her bag and putting them in his breast pocket. Why? Who on earth would do this on finding a decomposing body? It really does smack of a hindsight alibi to explain the dropping of the dart.

The tabloid could really have had a sensation on its hands if it had known that the real reason Stillwell was in the park was to expose himself to the little girls and that he was in the habit of alfresco masturbation on impulse. Those in Arundel who knew of Stillwell's predisposition to indecent exposure must have been horrified by him profiting from the 'gutter press' whether they believed him guilty of murder or not.

By opening himself up to the *Sunday Pictorial* like this Stillwell must have really believed this *was* the end of it all, guilty or not guilty, but what he did not know as he recounted his story to the hungry *Pictorial* reporter was that Jacks' dossier had hit desks in lofty offices, and a decision had been made in late February of 1950 to reopen the case. As Tom Stillwell and his family nervously read the exclusive in the paper that Sunday morning in Foxes' Oven, they would not have known that the legendary Inspector Spooner of the Yard was poised to arrive in Arundel.

12
THE GREAT DETECTIVE

Reginald William Lockerbie Spooner was born in Lambeth, London, in 1903. He was the son of Jabez Spooner and grandson of one Alfred Spooner. His grandfather had shot himself dead following a run of fiscal bad luck with investments that plunged him into bankruptcy. Spooner's father Jabez had also lost *his* smaller fortune when his business floundered after he became ill. These financial disasters cast a shadow over the Spooner family history and mindset. Money was scarce when Reginald was born, and the worry about getting it and holding on to it was genetically imprinted on the young boy.

A great-grandfather on his mother's side, Jeremiah Lockerbie, was one of the first of Sir Robert Peel's Bobbies – Peelers, as they were known – who between 1838 and 1852 made up the first professional police force in London. It was this tenuous historical connection that helped Reg (as he was commonly known) get accepted for the police force in 1924. Having seen and felt the monetary tribulations of his ancestors the prospect of stable employment with a salary and lifelong pension seemed immensely appealing.

By the time he joined the Metropolitan Police he was a handsome man of 6 foot 1, weighing 11 stone 8 pounds. He was fit and played a high standard of football and competent cricket. He smoked heavily – indeed, in later years colleagues joked that a cigarette was surgically attached to his lower lip – but in those days most men did. The day he was up before the selection board and was told he would be informed by letter of their decision another young hopeful approached him and suggested they went to the pub together for a drink. His name was Fred Narborough. They were to become colleagues and, perhaps, rivals.

Spooner's first post as a young constable was in Victoria Park, Hackney, then considered a bit of an outpost as far as crime was concerned, and the new policeman fretted that he might find it difficult to shine. Times have changed. Narborough, who was at the busier Hackney main station, and Spooner were already ambitious, and a year after becoming policemen both men applied to join the CID as detectives. Narborough got into plain clothes at the first time of asking, but Reg Spooner had to wait nearly a year longer. He always believed his height and the conspicuousness that it brought with it counted against him. Yet he flourished once he became a detective, soon building a reputation for diligence and persistence combined with a flair for knowing how the criminal mind worked. Surprisingly, for such a young man, he quickly assembled a coterie of productive informers – grasses and snitches as they were more colloquially known.

Confident that his career was on course, and having already cracked some newsworthy cases, Spooner married his longtime sweetheart Myra in 1929, and their only child Jean was born the following year. In 1933 he was promoted to detective sergeant on a good wage of £6 a week, and the following year his rite of passage was complete when John Frederick Stockwell, a teenager who murdered a cinema manager in Bow, London, became the first man to be sent to the gallows as a result of Spooner's efforts. Stockwell was a nineteen-year-old usher at the Palace Cinema in Bow who re-entered the cinema after closing and battered his manager to death while stealing the takings.

In 1938 Reg was elevated again to detective inspector, but during the Second World War Reg Spooner was seconded to MI5 where, among other things, he worked in the West London Aliens Tribunals. His task was to interview 'aliens' living in London and decide whether they were anti-British or a threat in any way and, if considered so, have them locked up for the duration of the war. He was later commended for securing the highest number of internments of any officer.

He then moved on to working in France and eventually Germany on top-secret anti-espionage and anti-sabotage work. (Interestingly, the three policemen or ex-policemen at the centre of this case – Narborough, Spooner and Jacks – all spent some of their careers in Germany.)

After the war Spooner returned to normal police duties after attaining the rank of major in the Intelligence Corps and was also now a divisional detective inspector at Scotland Yard, having been promoted in his absence.

In June 1946 he became involved in the most famous case of his career and one that would make him a household name.

Spooner, then based at Hammersmith Police Station, was called to the Pembridge Court Hotel, Notting Hill Gate, to view the dead body of a lady named Margery Gardner. She had been badly beaten and murdered. Her nipples had been almost bitten off, she had been horse-whipped and a rough instrument had been thrust into her vagina. Both the hardened policeman and the pathologist, Dr Keith Simpson, were shaken by the sexual savagery on display. It did not take Spooner long to suspect that Margery Gardner was a sado-masochist and the man he was looking for was a confidence trickster by the name of Neville Heath masquerading as a distinguished airman. He had signed the hotel guestbook, and a fingerprint of his was identified in the hotel room.

A huge manhunt was launched, and before Heath was finally apprehended, posing as a Group Captain Rupert Brooke, he managed to slay another young lady, Doreen Marshall, in Bournemouth. A phone call from a hotel worker, suspecting Brooke was indeed Heath, sent Spooner down to Dorset, and he was arrested. He was executed on 26 October 1946 by Pierrepoint. Sharing a drink afterwards policeman and executioner exchanged notes. Pierrepoint told Spooner that the Prison Governor had offered Heath a whisky before the noose was to be placed around his neck.

Heath accepted and added, 'Better make it a double.'

The fame and acclaim that Spooner garnered from this case must have had more to do with the horror of Heath and his crimes, which captured the public imagination, than any great feats of detection. As we have seen, the trail to the murderer's identity was rudimentary, and the fact that their target managed to kill another victim while the manhunt was in progress can hardly be labelled as a good result. His next seriously high-profile case was that of Joan Woodhouse, and Spooner, as we will see, came up with his own theory as to why he was unable to solve that one.

In January 1949 Reg Spooner had been made chief inspector and six months later upgraded again to detective superintendent. His rise through the ranks was gaining momentum, and his place in Scotland Yard history already assured. On Sunday 19 February 1950 he caught the early-morning train from London to Littlehampton where he had decided to base himself while investigating the eighteen-month-old murder of Joan Woodhouse.

From Littlehampton he called his friend Fred Narborough, now ex-Scotland Yard, out of courtesy. Spooner told him it was best they did not converse about the case until after his new investigation was complete, as he wanted to approach it with a fresh mind. Narborough must have felt apprehensive about this development. He and Spooner had joined up together, and although he, Fred, had nosed ahead in the early years in the career stakes, Reg had overtaken him. Now his ex-colleague and chum was being moved on to the case that was his biggest failure – one that may have ended his career – and, perhaps, solve it, emerge triumphant again and sully Fred's reputation further in the process.

Joan's family's understandable excitement and soaring hopes at this development were severely tempered by a small article that they read in their leading regional newspaper. On 1 March 1950 the *Yorkshire Post* said that 'reliable sources' indicated that there was little hope of an arrest being made after resumed inquiries. Who were these reliable sources, and how could they make this statement when the new inquiry had not begun? Later, that small item would be seen by the family as more evidence that the result of Spooner's reinvestigation was preordained. The reopening of the case was more about public relations than a renewed effort to solve a crime or a search for justice, they believed.

13
AN INSPECTOR CALLS
(AGAIN)

Inspector Spooner spent six weeks in Arundel and returned to Scotland Yard permanently in April 1950. In that time he had re-interviewed the original witnesses and the new ones uncovered by Thomas Jacks. He also probed Thomas Stillwell who recalled in a newspaper interview that the Scotland Yard policeman was an 'absolute gentleman', which suggests he may not have felt the same way about Narborough.

He presented his report to the DPP towards the end of May 1950 and assumed that would be the end of it. The key finding he made was that there was no evidence to justify the arrest of Thomas Stillwell on any charge concerning the death of Joan Woodhouse. There was no mention of any other suspects or any plans to find any. The DPP digested Spooner's report and a few days later issued an official statement saying that nothing had resulted from the second investigation that could justify further action.

It is bizarre that they all reached this decision, because Inspector Spooner's report *does* lay out evidence that was not presented by Narborough and had been unearthed by Thomas Jacks. Although the report was written at the close of Spooner's investigation it was not made available to the Woodhouse family, who would have found much of it interesting and a great help in their future private prosecution.

The report reveals that in 1950 the doctor who had treated Stillwell was interviewed, and he confirmed his patient had come to him with a poisoned finger. There is no comment in the report as to why the doctor was not interviewed in 1948 when memories would have been fresher. Also Jacks had assembled a number of witnesses supporting Phil Challen's assertion that he saw Stillwell in the park on the Saturday afternoon of the murder, undermining his friend Clement's belief they were in the park in the morning.

The report also makes reference for the first time to Mrs Stillwell, Tom's mother, taking her washing across town to her sister-in-law Dorothy Butcher's house for her to do shortly after the murder. Spooner concluded that this was quite innocent and that Mrs Stillwell was merely reducing her housework burden. It was confirmed, however, that this arrangement did begin just after the murder.

Perhaps, most damningly had it been publicly available, was the revelation that Stillwell had exposed himself to an eleven-year-old local girl, Beryl, only days before the murder. He jumped out on her in an aroused state and scared the girl who was able to run away and report the incident to her parents. They knew who Stillwell was, and although the family complained to the Stillwell family they did not go to the police. When Spooner interviewed them in 1950 mother and daughter confirmed the incident.

Despite this pointing to Thomas Stillwell being in a sexually excited and reckless state around the time of the murder and around the vicinity of the murder site, this information was not released to the family or their legal teams mounting a private prosecution. It also begs the question as to why Thomas Stillwell was not charged with indecent exposure.

Furthermore, there was another witness Spooner was obliged to interview. A lady named Johnson, who also knew the Stillwell family, made a statement reporting that Stillwell had jumped out on her by the River Arun and said menacingly, 'I want to strip you and throw you in that river for a swim.' If believed, proven or admitted this shows that Stillwell was harbouring thoughts of sex and violence.

The Woodhouse family and Thomas Jacks were again devastated by Spooner's recommendations not to charge Stillwell. They really believed that with Narborough out of the way Scotland Yard would be satisfied by having the errors of the first investigation shouldered by the ex-detective and would now get on with the business of pursuing justice. They had all read Jacks' report and could not see how anyone neutral or with an ounce of intelligence would not say that the evidence that did exist was not worthy of scrutiny in a courtroom. Circumstantial it may have been, but the sheer weight of it deserved judging. In their eyes the decision beggared belief.

Thomas Jacks was now past being worried about offending members of his old profession. He demanded an interview with Inspector Spooner and was granted it. It is not known what passed between the two men, but one could imagine it was a difficult encounter between the down-to-earth, bluff Yorkshireman and the quiet, cautious but determined Londoner. Jacks said later he was told, off the record, that there might be sufficient evidence to arrest a man but not to make his conviction secure.

'What right has a policeman to decide whether evidence is sufficient to get a conviction? The conviction of any accused person is in the hands of the judge and jury, NOT THE POLICE,' he thundered to the *Reynold's News*.

He continued to rail against Scotland Yard, his anger culminating in a direct threat. 'Tell the people this. For some unknown reason the authorities are refusing to co-operate. But, come what may, we shall follow and fight this thing through until we either win or lose. I am confident we shall win. To Scotland Yard I say . . . either you arrest and prosecute or I will.'

He stopped short of saying how. This was no longer a routine paid private detective job: Spooner and Scotland Yard had undermined Thomas Jacks as a professional and as a person. He was raging.

In a letter to the DPP written on 28 September 1950 Jacks complained bitterly about the behaviour of Detective Superintendent R Eagle, of West Sussex CID, Chichester. Eagle, he contended, had completely ignored the new evidence that Jacks had presented even though he had asked to see it as Jacks uncovered it. He argued that the Chamberlain evidence alone was enough for West Sussex CID to charge Stillwell. Instead they sent for Spooner. When the case reopened under Spooner they did not consult or interview Jacks. If the three parties had worked together instead of against one another he is sure the case would have been solved.

He also complained about Eagle, telling the *Yorkshire Post* (because that newspaper, he believed, was one of the 'reliable sources' cited) the case had been shelved as unsolved before the DPP had even received Spooner's report. He also referred to a Superintendent Catt of Littlehampton police telling the press that the case was going to be thrown out before it had finished, before even Chamberlain had given evidence. How could he say this with confidence?

John Woodhouse had also been appalled to read in his *Yorkshire Post* that the case was closed. This bothered and dismayed him because this statement was made before the DPP had made their announcement and before Spooner had delivered his report. It was wrong that he should say this before the family had been informed and even more wrong if he knew what the outcome was going to be before the DPP had officially made a decision based on Spooner's findings. He wrote a strong letter to Sir Hartley Shawcross, the attorney general:

> I am dejected and dispirited . . . No one has yet answered the question . . . why the person who was suspect was not brought for questioning when he was first suspected? We have a deep conviction that because this was not done we have been deprived of justice.

Shawcross replied in due course. 'I deeply sympathise with you, but am unable to add anything further.'

Ida and Annie wrote their own letter:

> The authorities have made a colossal blunder by not being prepared to accept the overwhelming evidence available of Joan's character and way of life. As the Vicar of St Mary's Church, Bryanston Square, said: 'Joan achieved more spiritually in her 27 years that many another at 80. She was one of the finest girls I have ever met.'
>
> Joan was killed because she fought to defend her honour, showing by this that she lived not only as a Christian, but could die like one. Could she have compromised with such an evil, as many less spiritually minded girls might have done, she would be alive today.

In another letter Ida wrote to the DPP on 19 May 1950, she said:

> It is almost incredible that in a so-called highly civilised country such treatment can be meted out and that there are men in authority who, in a case of this magnitude, will place prestige before right and honour.

The legal Establishment were immovable. They were accustomed to the pleas of the families of victims, but they were especially sensitive at this time to the possibility of a miscarriage of justice, especially as the public attitude to death by hanging was shifting radically.

A few weeks before, in March 1950, Timothy Evans had been hanged for the murder of his wife and daughter, and within a couple of years, following the arrest of serial killer John Christie, it would become apparent that he had been innocent. The hangings of Derek Bentley and Ruth Ellis, both considered miscarriages of justice, were only a few years ahead. If the police were expressing doubt about the guilt of a person the Establishment certainly was not going to overrule them and risk an innocent man being put to death by the government.

However, if the police believed that the family were about to bow to the might of the system they were mistaken. Around this time they had placed a notice in the in memoriam columns of some newspapers, it read:

WOODHOUSE, JOAN MARY – Always remembering with deep pride and love our darling taken from us July 31, 1948. She is now where evil cannot molest, near to the heart of God – Daddy, Mummie and Nida, Yorkshire.

In what he hoped would be final closure on the case Inspector Spooner travelled up to Bridlington by train on Wednesday 9 August 1950. He had with him some personal belongings of Joan's to return to the family, including clothing, the contents of her handbag, letters, her diary and the address book. He braced himself for a difficult meeting in the fourth-floor flat overlooking the sea.

Lena Bamber was staying with the aunts at the time. Sixty years later she retained a vivid memory of that day:

I said to Nida and Nan, John and Mr Jacks that I would make myself scarce as I was not family. Nida would have none of it.

'You are Joan's best friend,' Nida said, 'and as far as we are concerned you are family. No, you stay right here, you should hear everything the inspector has to say.'

Nida was the more strident one in the family. What she said went. Inspector Spooner arrived alone and was very polite, but I felt he was also very nervous. Nida, John and Mr Jacks all quizzed him, but he kept saying there was insufficient evidence, and they kept saying that was untrue.

Someone said if you don't think Stillwell did it then why are you closing the case and not looking for someone else. He could not answer this. When he was continuously pressed by us all he suddenly exploded. He made me jump as he slammed his clenched fist down on the table, his cheeks burning red, and snapped in a raised voice. 'Look, we all know Stillwell did it. Narborough failed in his investigation, and he's been sacked. He's gone. He's finished. So what more do you want?'

We were dumbfounded, to be honest, that the inspector thought we wanted some sort of revenge on Inspector Narborough. What more do we want? he asked. We want justice for Joan, that's all. That's what we said.

Mr Jacks told Inspector Spooner that we had no choice but to pursue the private prosecution. He didn't like that either.

It was a strange meeting all round. We all smelt drink on Inspector Spooner's breath, which we felt was unprofessional. We could only guess he had been drinking on the train journey up. In addition, and I know this sounds bizarre, he was wearing rouge on his cheeks and lipstick. I couldn't take my eyes off him. Perhaps, he knew his picture was going to be taken or maybe he had some sort of skin problem, but it all contributed to one of the strangest encounters of my life.

Spooner left the house after three tense hours and was met by some reporters waiting outside. He told them solemnly, 'No arrest is in sight. There are no fresh developments. We simply talked over the case. The private investigation is going on.'

The family wondered why Scotland Yard would have alerted the press to Spooner's visit. After all, it was a private and difficult meeting.

Inside the house a dispirited, angry and confused group of people reflected on the encounter. John Woodhouse sifted sombrely through Joan's returned belongings. He thumbed through Joan's address book and sighed heavily and then began to sob. He passed the book around, and all could see that each address had been crossed through roughly in pen, presumably as the police had eliminated each entry. The family thought that action was sadly indicative of the insensitivity to Joan's memory that had been shown throughout the case.

14
PRIVATE PROSECUTORS

Before the meeting with Inspector Spooner in Bridlington, the Woodhouse family along with Arnold Dickinson, the family's solicitor, and Thomas Jacks had explored what they could do next if the police persisted in closing the case a second time, and they finally concluded that the only route left to them was a private prosecution for murder to be brought by Joan's father. They had hoped that the very threat of such a legal device would have been enough to galvanise Scotland Yard and the DPP and that they would not have to carry it through.

On 4 August John Woodhouse and Thomas Jacks had been to see Mr Geoffrey Campbell, the Arundel magistrates' clerk, to apply for a warrant against Thomas Stillwell on a charge of murder. Mr Campbell said he could not issue a warrant and the case was problematical because it had been investigated by Scotland Yard and referred to the DPP. However, he was sympathetic and helpful and promised that he would consult a 'higher authority' and revert back to them.

The risks of pursuing a private prosecution were high. If the prosecution failed and new incriminating evidence emerged at a later date there would be no prospect of Thomas Stillwell standing trial for Joan's murder. Double jeopardy laws of the time dictated that nobody could be tried twice for the same crime.

In addition, the costs of mounting such an action were prohibitive, and the prospect of failure could lead the party that brought the action open to a lawsuit for malicious prosecution, and unlimited damages could flow from that potentially.

On top of this the chances of success were limited. For all the above reasons there had only been one such case previously in the United Kingdom, and there have only been two since. The most famous of these was during the 1990s when the family of the murdered black teenager Stephen Lawrence, disillusioned with the police inability to charge the young men they believed committed the racist murder of their son, launched their own high-profile private prosecution.

The only private prosecution prior to John Woodhouse's action had been nearly a century earlier, in 1865, when a distinguished and wealthy businessman, Henry Negretti, partner in Negretti and Zamba, world-renowned manufacturers of scientific instruments, prosecuted Gregorio Mogni for the murder by stabbing of Michael Harrington in the Golden Anchor pub in Saffron Hill, London.

On Boxing Day 1865 a fight had broken out in this pub owned by an ex-policeman between some Englishmen and a group of Italians, resulting in the death of Harrington. One of the Italians, Serafino Pelizzoni, who had been wounded, was accused of murder. Negretti somehow became involved in the case on hearing that Pelizzoni was innocent and indeed that he had been in another pub when the affray took place. It became clear to Negretti it was the cousin of Pelizzoni, Gregorio Mogni, who resembled him, who was responsible for the murder. The police chose to ignore Negretti's protestations and pressed ahead with their charge of wilful murder, and Pelizzoni was sentenced to hang.

Negretti was appalled that an innocent man was about to be executed and sought out Mogni from whom he obtained a confession. Despite having Mogni repeat his admission to a superintendent at King's Cross Police Station the police still did not act on it. Negretti resorted to making a citizen's arrest of Mogni and launching his own private prosecution.

Evidence that had been ruled out as hearsay at the trial of Pelizzoni could now be told, and new eyewitnesses identified Mogni as the man who had wielded the knife. Negretti was successful, and Mogni was committed for trial at the Old Bailey on the same charge of wilful murder, which was later amended to manslaughter. Mogni was found guilty and sentenced to five years' imprisonment and Negretti was commended by the court for his public-spirited action. The police and the legal authorities were seriously rebuked for their mistake and intransigence. John Woodhouse was aiming for a similar outcome.

However, it stood to reason that the legal Establishment, the government even, would not want this or any other private prosecution to succeed. If the plaintiff were successful it undermined the police and their role in the system. The floodgates could open and the largely functioning law, order and justice system would be fatally weakened. If the public prosecution route was seen as accessible to every person dissatisfied with a police investigation there could be hundreds of cases each year.

It *was* on the statute book but only for show. It was not intended to be used. The Woodhouse family had raised the stakes about as high as they could go. Desperate people will adopt desperate measures.

On the penultimate day of August 1950, following Inspector Spooner's visit, the negative replies from the DPP and after hearing nothing back from Geoffrey Campbell, the Magistrates' Clerk at Arundel, John Woodhouse, accompanied by Mr Dickinson and Mr AW Stephenson, a barrister from Hull, headed south on a train. Five Arundel magistrates at the boardroom of Littlehampton Harbour Board were expecting them.

Before presenting themselves at the seaside town they stopped at Arundel and walked into Arundel Park alongside Swanbourne Lake and climbed the steep hill up to Box Copse. It was a poignant moment as a father surveyed the very ground on which his much-loved daughter, his baby, had met her violent death. On the walnut tree, against which Joan had kicked, could be seen the neatly carved initials JW below a cross that had been inscribed by Ida and Annie on a previous visit. The small party stood, heads bowed, for a few sombre minutes before descending the hill.

By chance it was Carnival Week in Littlehampton and Arundel, and bunting and decorations hung across the streets of both towns. Arundel was experiencing a tourist boom, and there was no doubt that the events surrounding the murder had contributed to the spike in visitors. John Woodhouse was not the only man visiting Box Copse that day. Hotels were reported to be fully booked and tradesmen were gleefully counting record takings. One boatman complained to the *Reynold's News*, 'Trouble is, if the suspect is arrested and sent for trial it will be at Lewes. Then all our trade will be switched there.'

The same newspaper claimed that the town was equally divided between those who believed that the suspect was guilty and those that believed Joan had been murdered by a companion who had accompanied her to Arundel. Heated rows were being had in the saloon bars of the Norfolk and Bridge hotels as well as in the public bars of the working-men's public houses. One landlord said that if a certain local man was named he would throw the person who named him out on his ear. The majority, though, said the paper, just wanted the uncertainty and the cloud of suspicion to be lifted and for the ghoulish tourists to leave the town.

The three Yorkshiremen arrived in Littlehampton and demanded a murder warrant for Thomas Stillwell under the Indictable Offences Act of 1848, and Mr Dickinson firmly pronounced, 'Scotland Yard has refused a request to allow me access to the dossier on its murder investigations. I am dissatisfied with the reply, and I have asked that Mr Arthur Moody, MP for Gateshead East, approach the home secretary. If the warrant is not granted we shall apply to the King's Bench for a writ of mandamus.'

A writ of mandamus is where a superior court commands a subordinate court to take action. The Arundel magistrates took the view that the Wood-house family could no longer be resisted, or if they were to be the magistrates did not possess the powers to do so. After three-and-a-half hours of evidence taken behind closed doors, at 5.50 p.m. the first privately prosecuted murder warrant document for eighty-five years was drawn up, signed by magistrates Ernest West and Arthur Greaves and handed to Detective Sergeant Cowley of the local CID. John Woodhouse and Thomas Jacks' eyes followed Cowley out of the courtroom, both feeling now that the tide was turning in their crusade for justice for Joan.

Detective Inspector Dixie Dean had been recalled from holiday to be present should this eventuality materialise. He and Detective Sergeant Cowley took a car and drove from Littlehampton the six miles across country to Arundel, down Mill Road passing the Castle on the left, reaching the Black Rabbit on the right and climbing the hill to the hamlet of Offham. A gaggle of reporters followed in taxis and cars. The policemen parked their car by a stile next to a cabbage field and picked their way down the steep pathway (vividly described by Michael de Larrabeiti) to Foxes' Oven. They knocked on the door that was slightly ajar, pushed it and walked in.

Thomas Stillwell was sat at his kitchen table eating his tea having returned from a day's work in nearby Slindon. He was not surprised by the visit as he was well aware what was going on down in the town. He had told workmates he was not scared. 'An innocent man has nothing to be frightened about,' he declared.

Thomas asked if he could change from his work clothes and went into his bedroom and put on some grey flannels and grabbed a mackintosh, as there was heavy rain and a dark, threatening sky outside. When he came outside the cottage, at 6.15 p.m., he saw the shadows of the peering press posse at the top of the slope and wrapped the mackintosh around his head and shoulders to obscure any identifying photographs, which caused him difficulty in climbing the escarpment, which the rain had rendered treacherous.

The *Daily Express* captured the scene. Tom Stillwell made the front page, even if he was hidden by the raincoat. Detective Sergeant Cowley walks in front of him, casual and unperturbed with a pipe hanging languidly from his mouth, and Detective Inspector Dean brings up the rear, hands in pockets. The headline was 'Joan: Arrest on private warrant'. It had taken some time, but the murder victim was now being referred to by her Christian name only, not Joan Woodhouse or Arundel Murder Victim or the Bloomsbury Librarian. The media had, at last, decided that Joan was a worthy victim, deserving of their readers' sympathy.

On Thursday morning, 31 August, Thomas Stillwell, who had spent the night in the police cells at Littlehampton, appeared before Mr Ernest West at the magistrates' court. The arrest warrant was read to him, and Stillwell responded, 'I can only say I am innocent.'

Vincent Jackson, solicitor for the accused, stood up and applied for bail. 'In circumstances such as these you may think it is unusual, but the whole of these proceedings, to put it mildly, are rather unusual; in fact, perhaps, unheard of before.

'You have to consider whether Mr Stillwell is likely to run away. The whole of Sussex has known about this case for two years, yet my client has carried on with his work all that time.

'For over two years inquiries have been going on, and you have the fact that this man has made no attempt to run away.'

Superintendent Catt for the police responded, 'With every desire to be fair to the defendant it is my duty to strongly oppose bail.'

Mr West remanded Stillwell in custody until the following Friday. This young countryman had rarely ventured outside of Sussex, his home county, and this would be his first overnight stay in London. He was given a light lunch at Littlehampton Police Station before being put in the back of a police car and driven the fifty or so miles to London and finally through the forbidding medieval-looking gates of Brixton Prison.

It would have been a shocking and frightening experience for young Tom, having never experienced a prison before. A former criminal – known to the author, and who has led a blameless life for the past fifty years and would like to remain anonymous – who spent some time in Brixton Prison just a few years before Tom, describes his memories:

> We were made to bathe on arrival, but as remand prisoners were allowed to wear our own clothes afterwards. Also, I had my own cell. People could bring in food and fags, but as there was not much around during the war they tended not to. Meals were heralded by a jangling of keys and the appearance of a tray being pushed along the floor by a screw's shiny shoe. In the morning and the afternoon we were allowed outside for exercise – we walked like hamsters on a wheel around the edge of the yard. By far the most unpleasant side, for me at least, was the slopping out. We had to piss and shit into a pot which would fester and steam during the night until we were allowed to empty the foul contents into communal toilets in the morning. I remember we were allowed to borrow one book from the library and I would read up until lights-out at 9 p.m.

That night as Tom pulled the coarse blanket up to his chin in his stinking cell, surrounded by dangerous and often hopeless men, he must have wondered if his days were now truly numbered.

15
COMMITTED?

The committal proceedings were set to begin at Arundel Town Hall, suitably adapted to hold the case, on Tuesday 19 September 1950. These proceedings would be to decide whether the case was sufficiently strong to be put before a full court with a jury. In effect this would be a rehearsal for the trial, with defence barristers present to challenge arguments and cross-examine witnesses.

Crucially, law dictated that the prosecution of the case would be taken over by the State – that is, the Crown. This could be seen as a built-in inherent flaw (or device) that would always render a private prosecution for murder difficult to win and likely to fall at this hurdle. The prosecuting team are working for masters who have resisted the case thus far. To put in more emotive and simple terms – their hearts are unlikely to be in it.

Mr Edward Robey first explained that the DPP had taken over the case following the private prosecution launched by Mr John Woodhouse. The actual Director of Public Prosecutions, Sir Theobald Mathew, had already informed Mr Arnold Dickinson, the family's solicitor in Hull, that under the Prosecution of Offences Regulation, 1946, it was the DPP's duty to carry out the prosecution.

He had also made a special request that any information or evidence which was not already in possession of the police should be handed to Inspector Spooner. As we shall see, the police did not reciprocate. Mr Dickinson told his local newspaper that the DPP would take over the prosecution costs, and he also told the *Daily Mail* that the DPP should reimburse the aunts all their inquiry costs, including Thomas Jacks and his own solicitors' bill of £100, as it was the private inquiry that had led to the prosecution.

Sir Theobald Mathew would go on to become the longest-serving DPP to date, not relinquishing his post until 1964, following a twenty-year tenure. Ten years after the Arundel murder case he would be responsible for authorising the prosecution of Penguin Books for obscenity after they had published *Lady Chatterley's Lover* by DH Lawrence. His ruling ensured that Lawrence's rustic and erotic novel about an aristocrat's passionate affair with the estate gamekeeper would sell millions of copies and achieve international renown. He had been a noted barrister in his earlier career, and his wry remark that 'Justice is open to all – like the Savoy Grill' is often referred to when he is recalled.

Mr John Stuart Bass was appointed lead prosecuting lawyer for the DPP. He was a 45-year-old married man with four teenage children. Assisting him was the aforementioned Edward Robey, who enjoyed a higher profile chiefly because he was the son of the celebrated music-hall comedian George Robey and resembled him in looks.

Robey senior was one of the most popular men in the country – for a period known affectionately to the public as the Prime Minister of Mirth after one of his stage characters. He raised vast amounts of money for the First World War effort, and in 1954, the year he died, he accepted a knighthood. George Robey was as famous in his pomp as a world without television and radio would permit. His song 'If You Were The Only Girl In The World' was on everyone's lips when it was first aired and for many years after. Today, most people still know the song. Robey junior was brought into a world of immense privilege, as his father earned phenomenal amounts of money, but the boy was evidently determined to be his own man and entered the legal profession.

Vincent Jackson, the local solicitor, would, again, be defending Thomas Stillwell.

Arundel Town Hall, in Maltravers Street, is a seventeenth-century Gothic-looking but welcoming building, and the improvised courtroom inside served to make the backdrop somewhat informal and parochial for what could be a historic hearing, one that commanded nationwide interest.

Matronly local women sat alongside ranks of reporters from the national press, notebooks at the ready, in the area set aside for the public. The town hall was more accustomed to conducting tedious council meetings and whist drives, and as recently as the previous Saturday a dance had been held where now a yellow prefabricated dock had been pushed into position. This was all on the first floor. Below, at ground level in a room normally used for civic suppers, the thirty-five witnesses were gathered, waiting to be called. Among them was Fred Narborough, now no longer a policeman or a security adviser in Germany but a shareholder in a public house.

Outside, Stillwell had arrived in a car from Littlehampton Police Station, having been driven down from Brixton with a blind drawn across the back windscreen. Some uniformed officers took him from the car and allowed him to pull the mackintosh over his head again as they guided him up the steel fire escape into the back of the building.

Then, adding to the surreal feel of the proceedings, as soon as everyone had taken their seats that Tuesday morning the accused himself appeared, pantomime style, through wooden panelling in the wall. He stood upright facing the seated magistrates, three men and two women, looking almost insignificant in front of twelve-foot-high oil paintings of past dukes of Norfolk and an assortment of other mutton-whiskered former Arundel aristocracy. The seated magistrates were Ernest West, the chairman and an accountant by trade, Mrs Evelyn Emmet of Amberley Castle – who would later become a rare-for-the-time woman MP for the Conservatives in East Grinstead – Mrs G Allen-Williams, Mr CCG Roberts and Mr M Gosden.

Stillwell looked smart and dapper in a new sports jacket, flamboyant almost with a sprig of white heather pinned defiantly to his lapel. He later said this had been given to him by his fiancée to wear for luck. His three weeks in prison had not sapped him. Being on remand he had been able to wear his own clothes and accept food, drink and cigarettes bought to him by visitors. Remand is for the nearly guilty in the eyes of the system.

Tom smiled as a policeman handed him a notebook, and then he stepped back from the dock and sat down in front of it. He made no eye contact, but sitting within a few feet of him was Thomas Jacks, his potential nemesis, and John Woodhouse. The more observant spectators in the court noticed that Stillwell kept his fingers crossed throughout the day.

Mr John Stuart Bass, the prosecutor for the Crown, got to his feet and made an opening address that stunned almost everybody present. 'The evidence against this man is wholly circumstantial,' he declared. 'There is not one single piece of evidence which goes directly to show that he was a party to the commission of this crime. If the evidence does no more than

A portrait of Joan Woodhouse taken shortly before her murder in July 1948.

Joan in happier times: sunbathing, 1935 (top) – following her murder, Joan's fondness for sunbathing led some to question her moral character; in Folkestone, Kent, 1935, with her aunts, Ida Sherriff and Annie Blades, known as Nida and Nan (above right); at University College Library, London, 1947 (above left).

Above: The path through Arundel Park with the slope up to Box Copse – where Joan's body was found – to the right.

Left: The mock-up picture of Joan and how she would have appeared on the day of her murder issued by the police and published in the press.

Left: Thomas Stillwell, the local man who discovered Joan's body and who was later accused of her murder, seen here in his football kit.

Below: Foxes' Oven today, buried deep in the hamlet of Offham, West Sussex; in 1948 it was the home of the Stillwell family.

Bottom: The Black Rabbit, Offham, where Stillwell played darts after discovering Joan's body; the brewer's name is an eerie coincidence.

Left: John Woodhouse, Joan's father, had to face the murder of his daughter and a long battle for justice.

Below: Lena Bamber, Joan's friend (centre), with Joan's redoubtable aunts Nida (left) and Nan (right); the three women visited Arundel regularly after 1948 in their own pursuit of justice.

Above: Inspector Fred Narborough, the first Scotland Yard detective to be assigned to the 'Arundel murder' case.

Below: Inspector Reg Spooner (left), the second Yard detective to be assigned to the case, in conversation with Narborough (centre).

Criminal, Civil and all other enquiries of a confidential
nature.

Jacks' Private Detective Agency

T. P. Jacks.

10 Borough Road,
Bridlington, Yorks.
Tel. 4659.

Thomas Jacks, the private detective from Bridlington,
Yorkshire, who was hired by the Woodhouse family to
try to succeed where the police had failed.

Above: Reg Spooner at his desk; Spooner was a legendary Scotland Yard detective who, his colleagues said, had a cigarette surgically attached to his lip. He later wrote that he believed that Joan had committed suicide, despite the pathologist finding that Joan was raped and strangled.

Right: Spooner (left) with an unnamed colleague.

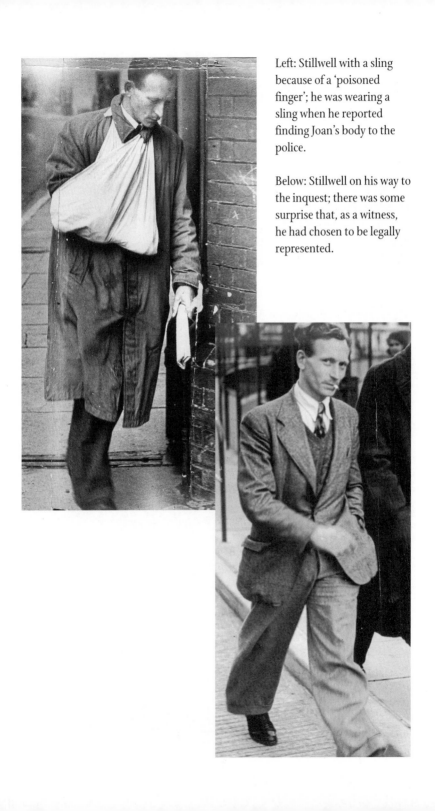

Left: Stillwell with a sling because of a 'poisoned finger'; he was wearing a sling when he reported finding Joan's body to the police.

Below: Stillwell on his way to the inquest; there was some surprise that, as a witness, he had chosen to be legally represented.

Above: Stillwell, now an official suspect, enters
Arundel Town Hall from the rear of the building
(seen below as it is today) for a hearing.

Above: Stuart Bass, the Crown's prosecutor, who bizarrely prefaced his case against Stillwell by saying, 'Never before in a charge of murder have you had less evidence.'

Left: Vincent Jackson, the local solicitor who represented Stillwell, arrives at the hearing at Arundel Town Hall.

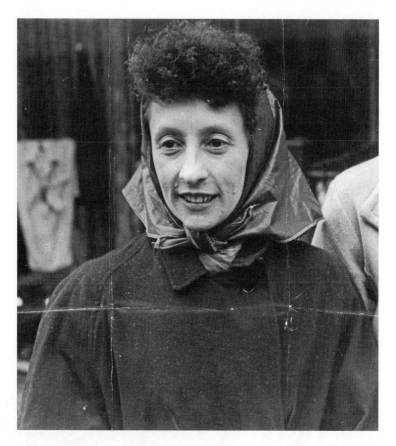

Above: Witness Mrs
Petley, who believed she
saw Stillwell in Arundel
Park walking alongside
Joan on the day of the
murder.

Left: Ellen Stillwell,
Tom's mother, and
Tom's brother Arthur
rush to the court.

Above: Jurors examine the crime scene around Box Copse.

Below: Stillwell sold his story to the newspapers after his case was dropped; this is one of the 'scoops', from the *Sunday Pictorial* of 26 February 1950.

Above: Bernard Marmaduke Fitzalan-Howard, 16th Duke of Norfolk and owner of Arundel Castle; a strong facial resemblance with Thomas Stillwell (opposite) led to local rumours of a family connection.

Left: Stillwell in middle age; he led a blameless life in Arundel for the rest of his days.

Below: A misty view of Arundel Castle from the Black Rabbit pub, Offham, 2015; it was in the grounds of the castle, to the right of the picture, where Joan's body was discovered.

to show that the defendant had the opportunity to commit the crime if he so desired, it would not be proper to commit him to trial.'

It was extraordinary that Mr Bass should open his remarks with this entreaty stressing the weaknesses of the Crown's case and pointing the magistrates to the decision he was making clear was the desired one. He could have taken the words straight out of the defence lawyer's mouth. It was a stunning declaration of intent or lack of it: a clear message that the prosecution team would be going through the motions but had no confidence that their case held any water – or were under instruction that it should not be won.

At this point John Woodhouse and Thomas Jacks must have felt like screaming or crying. Their only hope now after this dismal start must have been that either the weight of that circumstantial evidence would be sufficient to sway the magistrates or that something emerged during proceedings that would incriminate Stillwell convincingly. Perhaps he would incriminate himself?

It was always going to be a long shot after the mighty Crown had made it so abundantly clear to those small-town dignitaries what was expected of them.

16
THE OPENING SPEECH

Having undermined his entire case – the entire prosecution – Mr Bass went on to set out his stall and summarise the situation. It was clear he *was* going through the motions.

He said that a total of thirty-five witnesses would be called by the prosecution and then began his outline.

'At about 5.20 p.m. on 10 August 1948, Thomas Stillwell arrived at Arundel Police Station and reported that he had found a body at Box Copse in Arundel Park, a woman's body. He took police officers to the spot. But, at no time were the police, although they had the assistance of Scotland Yard, ever in a position to make an arrest or apply for process until August 30 of this year, when at the instance of a private prosecutor, the justices of this town issued a warrant for the arrest of the accused.

'Robbery as a motive seems excluded, as a diamond ring was found on one of the girl's fingers after death. In fact, from the examination made by Dr Keith Simpson, it seems clear that rape was the object of the attack. The doctor is satisfied that the cause of death was manual strangulation following upon forcible carnal knowledge or attempt at forcible carnal knowledge.

'The girl's clothing was spread out in a rather remarkable fashion. A raincoat was spread at the foot of some trees, and on it rested an overcoat which had been folded in the shape of a pillow. A dress was on the raincoat, and there was also found a brown sling leather handbag. An empty bottle which had contained a lemon-barley drink was found, and nearby there was a sleeping tablet in an envelope.

'It would seem as if this woman was surprised when she was lying on the clothing at the foot of the trees, having for some reason – difficult to imagine – removed her dress and had been strangled where she lay or had broken away from her assailant and run down the slope – where she was finally caught and strangled. That is only surmise. It is difficult to be sure, but that seems the most likely explanation of how this woman met her death.'

John Woodhouse was aghast that the prosecutor, his prosecutor, was using such language. 'For some reason difficult to imagine' – what was Bass playing at? He was meant to be on the family's side yet here he was casting innuendo and doubt, again, about Joan.

Bass continued.

'A dart was found at the scene, and this belonged to Stillwell, *but this has no bearing on what happened.*'

Again, Messrs Woodhouse and Jacks were perplexed that the man supposedly representing them would conclude on the magistrates' behalf that Stillwell's dart being found at the scene of the crime had no bearing on the case.

'When the body was found inquiries were made to ascertain how Miss Woodhouse came to be in Arundel Park at all,' Bass went on. 'On 31 July, which was the Saturday of the August bank-holiday weekend, a Miss Ashby, who was also a resident at the Blackheath hostel where Miss Woodhouse lived, saw Miss Woodhouse leave at 8.30 a.m. She was expected at Barnsley, her family home, that weekend. The next trace which could be found of her was at Worthing Central Station, where, about noon that day, someone deposited a blue travelling case. The person who deposited that case was given a ticket numbered 3007, and after Miss Woodhouse's body was found that ticket was in her bag.

'The next trace of her was at 2 p.m. A woman or a girl, not identified, visited a chemists' shop in High Street, Arundel, and bought a bottle of lemon barley drink. It is reasonably certain that it was Miss Woodhouse who made that purchase.

'At some time that afternoon a Miss Dibley, visiting friends in Arundel, happened to look out of the window and saw a woman in a striking blue dress walking in the direction of Mill Road, which goes into Arundel Park.

'There was one other piece of evidence indicating that Miss Woodhouse had gone into the park. A Mrs Petley, picnicing in the park with a Mrs Bidwell and their children, will say that she saw a man and a woman. She will say they were talking and appeared to be having words and she will say she identified the woman from photographs as Joan Woodhouse, and she says the man who was with Joan Woodhouse was the accused. On 14 September Mrs Petley picked out the accused at an identification parade.

'There is also evidence that Stillwell was seen in Box Copse in the immediate vicinity of the spot where the body was found. Two men, Mr Challen and Mr Clements, saw Stillwell walking towards a walnut tree. The explanation he gave was that he wanted to see if there were any walnuts. When it was pointed out to him that it was far too early for walnuts to be ripe, he said something about wanting to see if there would be any to gather later on. In a statement the accused has admitted meeting the two men at Box Copse. It is plain that this man had the opportunity to kill this woman if he so desired.

'Stillwell had an appointment in Arundel Square with a Miss Helen Egerton. It was an appointment she did not keep. However, it would have been possible for him to keep that appointment and get back to the park, and surprise this woman in Box Copse. Witnesses will confirm that the accused was seen cycling towards the town at 3.30 as if to keep the appointment with Miss Egerton, and at 4.20 his mother saw him cycling near the Black Rabbit public house. He told her he was going to the pictures in Littlehampton. She said he was wearing a grey jacket and grey flannel trousers. Mrs Petley had described the same clothes.

'The place where the body was found ten days later was something like a quarter of an hour's walk from the entrance to the park. It is not without significance that Stillwell entered the park at 4.30 and came out at 5 o'clock having found the body – with just sufficient time to walk to the spot and come back. At around 5.00 he saw his mother again.

'How did it come about that this man was able to walk straight up to the spot, return in half an hour and arrive at the police station at 5.30? It is a remarkable thing if the finding of the body was quite by chance. The magistrates might think the man who killed the woman on 31 July, and seeing nothing about it or the finding of the body in the press, could not restrain his curiosity any longer.

'He told a man named Chamberlain that he had found a body in Box Copse. When Chamberlain asked him what he was doing in the wood he said he had been to the doctor's. Witness will say that Thomas Stillwell remarked that he was sure foul play had taken place. This witness will be called, as will two little girls who saw Stillwell leaving Box Copse.

'Moving on to the opening day of the coroner's inquest, Stillwell met John Mobey on Arundel Bridge, and the conversation turned to the murder. He told Mobey that he had been to the inquest and that he had volunteered the information that he always went to the pictures on a Saturday. A week or two later he met Mobey in the cinema café. He sat down at Mobey's table and insisted on paying for his tea. What his motive was for getting into conversation with a man he really hardly knew and offering to pay for his tea is a matter for the magistrates to determine in the light of the other facts proved in this case.

'I suggest the answer might be that Stillwell was attempting to create an alibi by saying he always went to the pictures on a Saturday.

'And now I refer to the interviews between the accused and the police and the statements he was alleged to have made. Firstly, Stillwell was asked to give an account of his movements on 31 July 1948, and he said he was painting at home in the morning, went to an Arundel shop and in the afternoon went to Littlehampton and later visited the cinema there. He made no mention of having been in the park that day, and one does not know whether that was a deliberate omission.

'In a later statement he was alleged to have said that he was in the park on the Saturday, he saw a girl walking ahead of him, and he hurried to see if he could catch her up.

'"I walked up to the slope towards Box Copse in the direction the girl had taken," he said. "I saw she had turned around as she passed me. I spoke to her. I said, 'Good morning, lovely day.' I got no reply. She hurried down the slope. I walked on and whistled after her, but she did not reply. I sat down and later walked down to see if I could see her, but she had passed out of sight. I never saw her again. She seemed to be very nervous. She seemed to look at me and hurry on. The facial resemblance and the build of the girl I saw was similar to that of Joan Woodhouse.

'"I also saw another girl sitting on the bank. She waved to someone. I thought she was waving to me. I waved back, and then I saw she was joined by a man. There was a man using a pair of binoculars in the park."

'On the discovery of the body the accused has said in statements that he went to Box Copse because he thought he would be able to "knock over a rabbit" and pushed at several bushes and then saw the body.

'Stillwell also said, "I realised I had lost one of my darts. I could not find it on my allotment and other likely places, and eventually I went to the police station to see if I had dropped it at Box Copse. I last used these darts in the Black Rabbit."

'The accused also said, "Although all the facts seem to point to me, I am innocent and know nothing whatsoever about the death of Miss Woodhouse."

'On seeing a photograph of Joan Woodhouse Stillwell began to cry and said, "I suppose I am to blame for what happened to her. If that was the girl I saw I may have frightened her in the copse. It has been worrying me about that girl."

'We will demonstrate that the accused certainly told two lies. Lie number one refers to a short cut Stillwell claimed to have taken through the park when he discovered Joan's body. That was simply not true . . . and lie number two relates to the discovery of the girl's body. Stillwell told Mr Chamberlain that he had found her after a visit to the doctor's. If he had been to the doctor's he would have entered the park through another lodge.'

Mr Bass paused and addressed the magistrates directly.

'You will have to decide if there is evidence that this man not only tried accosting the woman but slew her in the wood that afternoon.'

He sat down, his opening speech having lasted ninety minutes.

After two police witnesses had produced a map, plans and photographs, Joan's father then entered the witness-box. He was shown a multicoloured Paisley dress and told Mr Bass he had never seen his daughter wearing such a dress. He confirmed that he was expecting Joan in Barnsley that weekend and that she would normally stay with him or her aunts when she returned home from London.

Dr Keith Simpson – balding, assured and distinguished – took the stand. Stillwell seemed transfixed by his presence, newspapers reported, and listened intently to his evidence. The pathologist reiterated his theory about how Joan had died resisting forcible sexual intercourse. He explained the body was clothed in underwear, stockings and shoes. He said that cuts and bruises to her lower legs indicated to him that she had been running through the undergrowth before being strangled.

Vincent Jackson, for the defence, made the point to Dr Simpson that there was no evidence of Joan's arms being forcibly held. 'Is it not a fair inference that her arms would be free to strike and scratch?'

'This does not necessarily mean that the arms were free, they may have been entangled in clothing,' countered Dr Simpson.

'Was the girl a virgin before the assault?' asked Mr Jackson, directly and unexpectedly.

'I cannot tell you definitely enough to help the court.'

Dr Holden, director of the Metropolitan Police Laboratory, followed and agreed with his colleague's interpretations of Joan's injuries. He also said that some hairs found on Joan's brassière did not come from Stillwell. This was a massive shock to John Woodhouse's team. It was the first time they had ever heard of any hairs being found on Joan's clothing. It was a piece of evidence that had not been shared with them. When were the hairs found? When was the sample of Stillwell's hair taken? Why had it not been shared with them until now? They were not in a position to challenge this as they knew nothing of it. Thomas Jacks and John Woodhouse both strongly felt something was not right about this development. (Dr Holden would later find himself in the public eye again when he gave evidence against the accused after the Great Train Robbery of 1963.)

Nicole Ashby took the stand. The attractive, black-haired young lady was obviously intimidated by the surroundings and the tragic situation in which she found herself. Nervously, and blinking rapidly as if to contain tears, she handled the remains of Joan's clothing, and holding her dress spattered with mud stains said, 'Yes, Joan was wearing this. It was a new dress.'

Mr Jackson cross-examined. 'Did Joan say where she was going that Saturday?'

'She said she was going home,' Nicole replied quietly, and the court was silent as several people contemplated the poignant finality of that statement.

17
'WITH TREMBLING HAND'

This signalled the end of the first day of the proceedings, and Thomas Stillwell sprang to his feet and waited to be escorted by police down the steel fire escape to a car outside. One press reporter observed that he showed no outward signs of fear and seemed to be absorbing the proceedings enthusiastically.

Joan's aunts had been aghast at Mr Bass's tack. Again, it appeared that the Establishment was more interested in blackening Joan's character than nailing the murderer. They composed a letter and delivered it to him before the court opened for business on the second day.

> Isn't it enough to know this girl died for decency and honour? She was a martyr of chastity. She could have lived if she could have compromised with the evil that overcame her but she chose to die rather than submit to that evil. I think you know this too. We are following the case and your attitude bewilders us. One day, if not on this earth, there will be a reckoning – that is inescapable.

A profound note indeed.

On the Wednesday morning the newspapers carried coverage of a spat between Clement Attlee and Winston Churchill over the nationalisation of the steel industry, but the story that excited the headline writers the most was about an enthusiastic milkman fined £2 by his trade union for delivering his goods too early. The *Daily Express*, however, revealed that John Woodhouse had adopted an eight-year-old girl 'to fill the gap caused by Joan's death'. Her name was Pamela, and John said the girl was helping him get through the ordeal of Joan's murder and its aftermath. Most of the other nationals ran an account of the first day of the Arundel hearing on their inside pages.

The court reconvened. The accused made his entrance through the panelled door after climbing the fire escape once again. He was wearing two white sprigs of heather now: the first from his fiancée that he had worn the previous day and the second given to him by his aunt, Nellie Butcher. One newspaper reported that the accused had become depressed the previous evening because his intended had sent him a note saying she would be unable to visit him at Littlehampton Police Station that night.

Mrs Nellie Victoria Petley, the first key witness, gave her evidence. She cut a pathetic figure on account of her voice having been reduced to a hoarse whisper by an attack of laryngitis. She told the court she had visited Arundel Park with her daily help, Beatrice Bidwell, and their children four or five times over the 1948 bank-holiday weekend.

'On the Saturday we went to a walnut tree near the end of Swanbourne Lake, getting there about two o'clock,' she said. 'We sat down near the tree. While there, I saw a young couple and two youths, about thirteen or fourteen years old.'

Mr Bass asked if the witness could see any of the persons from the park in the court. Mrs Petley fixed her eyes on Thomas Stillwell and nodded. She further identified two photographs of Joan Woodhouse as being like the woman she saw in the park.

'The two persons were coming up the path from the lake,' she went on. 'From a distance I noticed they were in conversation. Neither of them seemed very happy. I spoke to the man and asked him the time. He said he did not have it. The two passed me going away from the lake. They sat on the slope about 200 yards away – a substantial distance from me. I never saw them any more after the first few minutes.'

Mrs Petley confirmed that on 14 September this year she had attended a parade at Littlehampton Police Station and identified Stillwell from a number of other men as being the person she had seen in the park. She also confirmed that some weeks before this parade Mr Jacks had shown her some photographs, two of which she picked out as being the man she had seen in the park. Before that, though, she had seen a photograph of the accused in a Sunday newspaper.

Mr Bass then handed her a letter written on blue paper, which Mrs Petley confirmed was in her handwriting.

'I am putting it in as an exhibit although I am not entitled to read it,' explained the prosecutor, 'I put it in so that Mr Jackson should be in a position to ask questions about it.'

This was yet another example of the Crown strengthening the defence's case and served to make their conduct all the more bizarre.

Mr Jackson stood to cross-examine. Mrs Petley told him that she first gave information to the police two years ago. She had volunteered the information following appeals from the police in the newspapers. She said she had told them she had seen the couple in the park on 24 July, thinking that was the date of the bank-holiday Saturday. She was quite sure now it was 31 July.

Mr Jackson then read part of the blue letter – a letter Mrs Petley had sent to John Woodhouse and Thomas Jacks.

'It is with a trembling hand I write to you. I am an invalid with lung trouble, a young mother with three children. I will shock you, I know, but I am the last person to see Joan alive and the last one to talk to her.'

The defence lawyer proceeded to push Mrs Petley on this opening paragraph of her letter. He pointed out that she had earlier said she had spoken to Thomas Stillwell not Joan Woodhouse.

'I addressed them both together. She probably did not think I was addressing her.'

'But the only conversation you had was with Stillwell?'

'Yes, I spoke to Stillwell.'

'It is untrue then that you were the last person to speak to Joan?'

'Yes,' acknowledged Mrs Petley in a strained whisper. 'I meant I spoke to other people but not to Miss Woodhouse.'

'Then it is wrong for you to say in your letter that you were the last one to talk to her?'

'That was only in my mind.'

Mr Jackson paused for effect. He had scored points, but what it said about Mrs Petley's evidence, other than she hadn't ordered her thoughts meticulously, was not clear.

Mr Jackson progressed to Mrs Petley's confusion over the dates.

'I told the police that because I had made a mistake over my dates and because of this a murderer may go free. If you get the detective who took my statement you will find that I accurately described Joan and her frock before it was published. I said I saw them on the Sunday against my better judgement. I had told the police it was Saturday and they had taken no notice of my evidence. They said they had got an account of Joan's movements on the Saturday, and the papers said she was in Worthing on the Saturday night. I knew I was right and the police were wrong. When I saw Mr Jacks he straight away mentioned about the Sunday in the letter, and I told him then it was the Saturday.'

'Did you not alter your opinion about the date after seeing Mr Jacks?' Mrs Petley refuted this.

'You say you went to the park frequently,' probed Mr Jackson. 'Could you say where you sat in the park on the Saturday before 31 July 1948?'

'Probably not,' conceded Mrs Petley. 'I never thought any more of the episode until I saw a picture of a chap in a Sunday paper. Then I saw those same eyes, those same staring eyes of the chap who was with Joan that afternoon.'

Mr Jackson jumped in at this point: 'Do you agree that before the publishing of the photograph in a Sunday newspaper that you knew a reward of £500 had been offered?'

'Yes, but I had been to the police before the reward was out.'

To hammer his point home Mr Jackson read from the letter a further extract where Mrs Petley said she had been lying in her hospital bed and thought she would claim the reward and go away and get well. The witness agreed that in August this year, 1950, she wrote the letter to Mr Jacks and Mr Woodhouse with the full intention of helping to find the murderer. Mr Jackson completed his cross-examination by turning to the identity parade of 14 September.

'I suggest you looked straight at Stillwell and said it was the man and never looked at anyone else at all?'

'I noticed him and looked along the line,' replied Mrs Petley.

The defence were finished with Mrs Petley. Their attempts to paint her as an unreliable witness had been only partially successful. She had been confused over the dates, but her reasons were credible. She *did* have the reward in mind, it seemed, but, as she stressed, she had been to the police initially long before the reward was offered and only a couple of days after the discovery of the body, and she did want this emphasised in court. The fact that she described Joan's clothing accurately before it had been made public is a hard fact to argue against.

Her home help Beatrice Bidwell was also vulnerable on some key facts, and it was she who followed Mrs Petley into the witness-box. She reiterated she was in Arundel Park 'on a Saturday in the last few days of July'.

She went on, 'It was the first occasion we had been as far as the walnut tree, and we did not go so far again. We sat down, and I saw a fellow and a girl approaching from the direction of Swanbourne Lake.'

'Can you describe the man?' Mr Bass interjected.

'Only by his staring eyes.'

Mr Bass put it to her that she had been unable to identify Stillwell at the identification parade of 14 September 1950, and she agreed. She was then asked to describe the woman she had seen in the park. 'So far as I can remember, she had a Hungarian frock on. I had wanted a dress of that style myself.'

She was shown Joan's frock and said the dress she remembered was similar. Under cross-examination by Mr Jackson, Miss Bidwell said the couple were walking arm in arm. He seized on this.

'Just now you said you were some distance from Mrs Petley, and so far away you could not be sure about the frock. How far away were you?'

'Within hearing distance.'

'How far were you?' Mr Jackson's voice was rising.

'Some distance up the hill.'

'How far?'

'About six or seven yards.'

'About six or seven yards?' barked Mr Jackson.

'Maybe or maybe not.'

'Do you realise you are giving evidence on a very important matter?' the defending lawyer boomed.

'I do, yes,' replied Miss Bidwell and suitably chastened she was told there were no further questions.

Frank Clements, a painter and decorator of Canada Road, Arundel, took the stand next. He nodded to Stillwell, and Stillwell smiled back. The accused had been drawing a detailed plan of Box Copse on his pad but turned his page over and began doodling. Answering Mr Bass, Clements said that he and the man named Phil Challen saw Stillwell, whom he knew quite well, in Arundel Park on the bank-holiday Saturday. He put the time at between 9.30 and 11 in the morning. They spoke to Stillwell about some walnuts, and then he went up the bank towards Box Copse.

Mr Jackson wanted to question the witness.

'May I suggest that the meeting with Stillwell was on Saturday 24 July and not Saturday 31 July?'

'It was the Saturday previous to the bank holiday. I don't know the date,' Clements replied.

Oddly, neither lawyer asked Clements if he meant the Saturday before the bank-holiday Monday or before the bank-holiday weekend.

Challen himself followed. He, too, was a painter, like Clements and Stillwell, and also lived in Canada Road. He was clear about it being the Saturday of the August bank-holiday weekend and added that he was with his six-year-old daughter. He described walking to the walnut tree and seeing and speaking to the accused.

'What time would it be?' asked Mr Bass.

'Sometime in the afternoon.'

'You are quite sure about that, are you?'

'Yes.'

'Did you see where Stillwell went?'

'He went into the Box Copse wood. The time was between 2 and 4.'

Challen was an assured witness, but Mr Jackson was on his feet and looking for a chink in his armour.

'You go into the park very frequently?'

'Yes.'

'Quite often on Saturdays?'

'Yes.'

'Where had you been the Saturday previous?'

'I cannot say.'

'Where were you the Saturday previous to that?'

'I cannot say.'

'Are you sure then it cannot have been the Saturday previous when you saw Stillwell?'

'Absolutely positive.'

It would be an unusual witness who could recall what he was doing on any Saturday two years before unless there was a specific reason to remember a day because something had happened.

Mr Jackson was undeterred: 'Are you equally positive it was the afternoon?'

'Yes.'

'Are you equally sure Clements was with you, because Clements says it was in the morning?'

'Yes, I know he says it was in the morning, but I say it was in the afternoon.'

'Whatever day and whatever time, Stillwell was alone?'

'He was alone.'

Mr Frank Bragger of Arundel said he was marking a competition game between two members of Arundel Bowls Club and thought it was on the Saturday before the bank holiday. He said that Stillwell rode past him and nodded. The game had started at 2.45 p.m. and finished at 4 p.m., so his sighting was sometime in that seventy-five minutes.

Young Helen Egerton, barely sixteen years old, took the stand. She confirmed she had had an appointment with Stillwell on 31 July and that she did not keep the rendezvous.

The twenty-fifth witness to give evidence was Ellen Agnes Stillwell, Tom's mother. She had walked to the court that morning from Foxes' Oven and had sat calmly in the witness room knitting a jumper until she was called. As she took the stand her son's eyes rested on her affectionately, and they smiled at one another. She was wearing a heather-mixture dress and a close-fitting black hat from which a feather darted upwards. A corner of freshly laundered white blouse broke out over a lapel of her dress. As she began to answer questions it was noticeable that her hands were trembling.

Mrs Stillwell told Mr Bass that her son was still at home when she left to catch the 12.45 p.m. bus to Worthing on 31 July 1948. At 4.20 p.m. she came back by bus to Arundel.

'Did you see your son then?' queried Mr Bass.

'I thought I did, but I wouldn't be certain.' She added that she believed she saw him cycling down the hill towards the Black Rabbit, and he told her he was going to the pictures. She next saw him that night, a bit later than 10.45 p.m. She also mentioned that she went to Worthing one hour earlier than she normally did.

Mr Jackson intervened. 'Is it not possible you came back one hour earlier?'

'It may have been earlier because I did not get what I wanted. It might have been 3.20 p.m.'

Mr Bass was not about to let this pass. 'What was your first recollection when you were asked about the time?' he insisted.

Mr Jackson was indignant and appealed to the bench, 'This is getting very near cross-examination, very near. And this is a prosecution witness . . . I object to the question.'

'The question is a perfectly proper one, and it arose out of your cross-examination.'

Both men were now speaking with raised voices. Mrs Stillwell appeared to falter in the stand, and a policewoman guided a glass of water to her lips. Her son seemed concerned and stood for a second or two as if to help her. One journalist later wrote that mother and son seemed to have a visible telepathy, as they searched each other with their eyes continually.

The magistrates ruled the question in order, and when Mr Bass asked it again Mrs Stillwell said, 'Four-twenty is my usual time.'

After the hearing Mrs Stillwell was allowed to spend half an hour with her son, accompanied by her younger boy Arthur, in a little interview room in Arundel Police Station.

After she had left Tom had much to think about. Tomorrow, Thursday, should see the conclusion of the case and determine whether he would be a free man or whether the spectre of the hangman was to come one terrifying step closer.

18

'NEVER BEFORE IN A CHARGE OF MURDER HAVE YOU HAD LESS EVIDENCE'

Thursday 21 September 1950 was to be the most dramatic day in the committal hearing thus far. The morning's papers, while recording the previous day's events in Arundel, were dominated by news of US Marines attacking Communist troops in Korea; Prime Minister Clement Attlee visiting the king to discuss Korea and other world events; and playwright George Bernard Shaw undergoing another serious medical procedure. On the sports pages the England football team to play Ireland in an upcoming fixture was announced; Billy Wright was captain, Alf Ramsey in defence and Stanley Matthews and Tom Finney in attack.

The first witnesses to give evidence were concerned with confirming Thomas Stillwell's movements on the day of 10 August 1948, when the suspect had reported discovering Joan's body. André Buller, the man who hired out the pleasure boats on Swanbourne Lake, was up first. He saw and spoke to Stillwell between 4 and 4.40 p.m. that afternoon and again at about five o'clock when he was talking to the the lodge-keeper at Swanbourne Lodge, Frank Ferris.

The lodge-keeper himself followed the boat-hirer into the witness-box. He said he saw Stillwell between 4 and 5 p.m. and that he was coming from the park along the path beside the lake. Ferris confirmed that the defendant had told him he had found a body in Box Copse and was going to the police.

'Did you see if he spoke to anyone when he went into the road?' asked Mr Bass.

'Yes. His mother.'

Frederick George Chamberlain, licensee of the Black Rabbit, was next. He said he saw Stillwell near the post office in Arundel between 5.15 and 5.30 p.m. He had his arm in a sling, and he told the publican that he had a poisoned finger or thumb. Stillwell then went on to say, 'That is not all my trouble. I have found a body in the park.'

He stated that the body was thàt of a woman, and Chamberlain asked if it was an old woman.

'"No, I think she was twenty-six or twenty-seven," Stillwell replied,' said Chamberlain.

Mr Bass then asked the witness if he had said what he was doing in the park.

'I believe he said he had been to the doctor's and was going back to his home across the park.'

Mr Jackson rose to cross-examine. 'When you asked if it was an old woman, I suggest that what he said to you was that he thought it was a young woman between eighteen and thirty?'

'No, I am almost convinced in my own mind that he said between twenty-six and twenty-seven.'

The court quietened, and a wave of sympathy and empathy filled the room as thirteen-year-old Gillian Edith Parker walked meekly to the witness-box. Her green-and-yellow school blazer, striped tie and little-girl fringe accentuated her innocence and situation – a sweet schoolgirl being thrust rudely into the dark recesses of the adult world, a world she could not yet fully comprehend.

Mr Bass gently took her through her evidence. She spoke of her visits to the park two years ago with her friend Brenda Ansell in the first few weeks of August. She could not be more specific about the date but clearly remembered seeing a man with his arm in a sling.

'Do you think you would know him again if you saw him?' said Mr Bass calmly.

'I don't think I would,' replied the girl.

'Would you mind looking around the court to see if there was anyone present who looks like the man?'

It was a moment of drama. The girl could not have known the typical layout of a courtroom and who were witnesses, defendants, reporters or members of the public. She had already stated that she most probably would not know the man. Her parents would have likely kept any press coverage or photographs about the case away from her. She had no axe to grind with any one. She was an untainted, unbiased witness. Her eyes moved around the court. The responsibility of what she had been asked to do must have weighed heavily upon her. She was old enough to be aware of how uncomfortable it would be to indicate the wrong man, and therefore the easiest reply would be to say there was nobody present she recognised. Her line of vision alighted on Thomas Stillwell sitting and smiling, the sprig of white heather protruding from his button hole. He was relaxed with one hand behind his head. Although this was court-room drama, nothing hung on it. He had never denied meeting these two girls on the day of finding the body.

Gillian Parker lifted her arm and pointed straight at him. 'I think it's that man over there.'

'There is a wood where you saw the man walking?' Mr Bass continued. 'Yes.'

She added that the man spoke to them, but she could not remember what he said and that she had seen him previously, a short while before, sitting on the grass bank.

Mr Bass: 'Was there any mention as to where you lived?'

'Yes. He asked us if we were down for the day and then where we lived, and we said Chichester.'

Mr Jackson cross-examined. He wanted to know if the man had told them not to go to Box Copse, and the girl replied she thought he did and that he said not to go there because of cattle.

Mr Bass concluded that as the defendant had confirmed seeing the two girls in his own statements there was no need to call Brenda Ansell.

During the break for lunch the magistrates elected to visit Box Copse and travelled there in two cars followed by press and photographers and flanked by police. A herd of Shorthorn cattle were shooed out of their way as they climbed the hill, and one magistrate, seventy-year-old Mr Roberts, gave up and leaned on his stick. The others sombrely examined the spot where Joan was found and especially the walnut tree, which had been referred to in evidence, while at a short distance Fleet Street's finest recorded the moments for posterity with notebooks and bulky flash cameras.

John Mobey was called to give evidence in the afternoon. He told how Stillwell had opened up a conversation with him on the day of the inquest and had, out of the blue, volunteered the information that he always went to the pictures on a Saturday, which struck him as strange. A week later he met him again at a café in Littlehampton and there was more talk of the murder, and Stillwell said he did not know where he was on the day of the murder. They then tossed a coin over who would pay for the tea.

Next up was ex-Inspector Narborough. After Mr Bass had taken him through his evidence Mr Jackson began his cross-examination. He quickly moved to the subject of Joan's address book.

'Did you find a diary?'

'Yes, sir.'

'Would it be fair to say that in the year 1948, up to August, it had a very large number of addresses?

'Yes.'

'Were many of those names male persons?'

'Pretty well all were names and addresses of male persons.'

Mr Jackson, having given strength to the possibility of an alternative unknown suspect, attempted to move swiftly on, but to the relief of John Woodhouse and Thomas Jacks Narborough himself intervened.

'With respect, might I assist you regarding the names and addresses of the male acquaintances? I interviewed every one of those persons. They were all members of a librarians' association of which Joan Woodhouse was honorary secretary.'

'Did you do that?' queried Mr Jackson, possibly miffed by the ex-policeman's clarification.

'I had it done.'

'Then it wasn't evidence,' commented Mr Jackson.

Mr Bass was on his feet. 'The contents of the diary are not evidence either!'

Mr Jackson resumed, attempting to recover the momentum, 'At the time the adjourned inquest was held, had you before you the whole of the evidence available?'

'At that time, yes.'

'And did you tell the coroner and members of the jury that you had not sufficient evidence to warrant any charge being made?'

'That is so.'

Mr Jackson now moved on to the statements taken from Thomas Stillwell conscious that they were potentially highly incriminating and wanting to discredit them in advance. He put it to Narborough that he had told Stillwell that Mr Challen and Mr Clements had said they had seen him in the afternoon of Saturday 31 July and therefore there was no point in him denying he was there. Narborough refuted this. The ex-policeman also denied that he or the suspect was particularly tired after the interviewing sessions of 19 and 20 October 1948.

Ex-Inspector Narborough left the witness-box relatively unflustered and was replaced by Detective Inspector Dean who went through the statements made by Stillwell in his presence. He stated how Stillwell had revealed that the real reason he had lied about being in the park was because of fears over his parents losing their tied cottage because of his poaching.

He went through how the suspect had said he whistled at a girl in the park and had identified her initially as Joan Woodhouse and how he had broken down and said he 'must be to blame for her death' and had then qualified this by saying he had scared her into the copse where she must have met her murderer. Dean added that Stillwell later said he did not think the girl he frightened was Joan. When asked why he had not told them earlier about seeing the girl in the park, Stillwell had said, 'It's been worrying me.'

In a later interview, Dean said, the suspect was certain he did not go to the park on the morning of 31 July but knew he was in the park that day, so it must have been in the afternoon. He also mentioned that after whistling at the girl and following her he saw a man with field glasses.

Mr Jackson pressed Dean on the 19 and 20 October interviews. Dean confirmed that on the 19th Stillwell arrived at the police station at 9.40 am and was there until 5.15 p.m.. He returned at 6 p.m. the following day and was kept there until 5.30 am.

'I want to make it quite clear, not suggesting anything improper was done, but I want to ask you, was he questioned from the time he arrived until he left by Inspector Narborough, yourself and two other police officers?'

'Yes, sir.'

'At that time, Inspector, were you a little tired and weary?'

'Yes.'

'Would it be fair to him to say he was absolutely exhausted?'

'He was tired.'

'Somebody during that evening supplied him with two cups of tea and a cake?'

'He was supplied with some food, but I cannot remember off-hand what it was.'

Mr Jackson had successfully scored the point from Detective Inspector Dean he could not from Narborough.

This, the thirty-fifth witness, was the final person to give evidence.

Mr Bass rose to his feet, and instead of summing up the prosecution case and urging the magistrates to commit Thomas Stillwell to trial he addressed the bench.

'That is all the evidence the Crown can put before you.'

Far from being a rousing call to urge the magistrates to pave the way for justice to take its course, the prosecuting counsel had effectively issued an apology for bringing the case at all.

Vincent Jackson, representing Thomas Stillwell, had ended that day's proceedings by saying that it was 4.40 p.m., and he did not think he would be able to finish his summing up until after 6 p.m., so the magistrates postponed his speech and their verdict until Friday morning.

Mr Jackson had the advantage, therefore, of the last word. Indeed, in the light of Mr Bass passing up the opportunity and duty to make a closing speech and draw all the threads of the prosecuting case together, he had *all* the words. The local solicitor made his case slowly and carefully as Stillwell sat calmly fingering the sprig of white heather still on his person.

He opened by stating forcefully that no prima-facie case for murder had been made against his client.

'It is now my duty to put before you my submission, which will lead, I hope, to you coming to the conclusion that there is no case to answer. This case comes before you in a way in which I am aware is unique.

'Mr Bass, in his opening, said to you that inquiries were made by the police for months, and at no time were they able to make an arrest or apply for a process until 30 August this year, when, at the instigation of a private prosecutor, the warrant was granted.

'Mr Bass also said that the evidence was purely circumstantial. It will be my respectful submission there is not any circumstantial evidence which could possibly lead to the conviction of this man.

'Never before in a charge of murder have you had less evidence.'

It was a bold assertion, but Mr Jackson cleverly cast doubt on whether there was really any *proof* that the murder actually took place on 31 July. He also artfully presented the fact that the police's decision not to bring charges was evidence of Stillwell's innocence in itself. If there was doubt about that in the magistrates' minds then all other evidence heard became weaker. He pointed out that Mrs Petley was not a new witness and that her final clarity could have been spurred by the reward. He stressed the difference between Mr Challen and Mr Clements, how one believed they saw the accused in the morning and the other in the afternoon, and he planted the seed of how Stillwell himself could have been coerced into saying things that could have been incriminating through excessive tiredness during the marathon interview sessions.

'What evidence has been brought before you to give any assistance in coming to the conclusion that this woman was killed on 31 July?' he challenged.

'She is supposed to have been carrying a mackintosh and overcoat,' he continued, 'and does it not occur to you that nobody apparently noticed this extraordinary thing of a woman on a sweltering hot day carrying an overcoat and mackintosh? Either the woman in the striking dress seen by eye witnesses was not Joan Woodhouse or somebody else was carrying her coat.

'Where did Joan eat her meal? It is possible she was going to the park with some companion for a picnic meal? It may well be it was a male companion.

'She told Miss Ashby she was going home that weekend. Either she told her she was going home when she had no intention of doing so, and it was a deliberate lie because she was going to meet someone else and spend the weekend with that person, or, alternatively, she left her home with the intention of going to Yorkshire but on her way met somebody else as a result of which she altered her mind and set forth to Worthing and Arundel.

'The only evidence you have in any way that connects Stillwell with this matter is the evidence of Mrs Petley and Mrs Bidwell. Mrs Petley has given evidence which under the circumstances you must think extraordinary. What reliance can be placed on a woman who has made three different statements?

'Different stories have been told as to whether Stillwell was in the park in the morning or the afternoon on the suggested day. On the afternoon of 31 July Stillwell said he went to Littlehampton and at about four o'clock bought a shirt for ten shillings and then went to the pictures. After coming from the pictures he went to a public house and played darts until closing time. The police, no doubt, made extensive inquiries if this were true.

'Now we come, perhaps, to the most vital part of all. Dr Keith Simpson says that this woman was sexually assaulted. Do not let us mince our words – raped – and raped in such a fashion that he [Dr Simpson] could not give any opinion as to her condition on that matter.

'Some man got in touch with that woman and had violent intercourse with her, but if it be true that it was against her will, surely this girl with no marks upon her arms whatsoever would have hit or scratched the man about the face. The police said it would be probable that people were on the pathway below, yet no shouts were heard.

'The hairs found on Joan's brassière were not Joan's. They were not Stillwell's either. The only conclusion they could come to was that the hairs must have come from the man who assaulted Joan Woodhouse and killed her.

'I invite you to say that in view of the presumption of innocence, which must always be before you, there is no evidence that this woman was murdered on 31 July 1948 and no evidence on which you can connect these two people together, and I ask you to say there is no case to answer,' concluded Mr Jackson before taking his seat. His closing speech had lasted eighty minutes.

The magistrates retired to consider their verdict. Within two hours they filed back into the courtroom. The defendant had been brought back into the court a few minutes earlier and sat on a chair in front of the dock. He took a glass of water from the solicitor's clerk's table and gulped a mouthful before gripping the rail and facing the bench. He was ready. At the back of the court members of the public crowded into the small room, some of them standing on chairs and craning their necks for a better view. The magistrates took their time sitting down, adjusting their seats and spectacles and adding to the atmosphere of tense anticipation.

'We are of the unanimous opinion that there is insufficient evidence to justify sending Thomas Stillwell to trial for the murder of Joan Woodhouse. We therefore direct that Stillwell be discharged from custody. The court awards forty guineas towards the defence costs and grants special costs towards the prosecution for Dr Simpson and the DPP . . .'

Whether Mr Ernest West was going to continue further is unclear as cheers and clapping from around the court had drowned him out. Stillwell allowed himself a broad smile and clasped Vincent Jackson's hand before going outside and shaking hands with various Sussex police officers before covering his head again with his raincoat and getting into a car driven by the son of Mr Jackson away to a Chichester hotel where a party had been arranged and financed by a Sunday newspaper.

19
POISON PENS

Vincent Jackson promptly released a statement to the press thanking the police for the way they had helped him in preparing his defence and for allowing him to interview Stillwell in custody. On his client's behalf he quoted a few brief words.

'Now I am a free man after two years of being pointed at and talked about as the man of the Arundel Park murder. Now that shadow has gone. I can go back home and resume my life and forget all this horror.'

The *Western Morning News* had managed to grab a few words from ex-Inspector Fred Narborough. 'I never had any qualms of conscience about it at all whatever. I considered I did not have enough evidence to make an arrest.'

Up in Bridlington Ida Sheriff and Annie Blades stepped outside their flat and addressed persistent reporters. 'Please do not think we have been actuated by feelings of revenge and hatred. While we were being crucified by suggestions that our pure-hearted, idealistic Joan had been of doubtful character the police investigations into her death were postponed. So we decided to spend the money, which was to have been Joan's, on a private investigation.'

Over in Barnsley a sickened John Woodhouse gave a brief statement. It had emerged that he left the court before the verdict had been announced and headed home. He knew what the outcome was going to be and that the whole committal had been little more than a charade and could not bear to be present when the man he believed to be guilty of slaying his innocent daughter was set free. He heard the news from intrepid reporters when he stepped out of the train from Arundel at London Victoria's platform 13.

'I shall fight on to find the murderer even if I have only a loincloth left,' he vowed with unintended melodrama.

The *Daily Graphic* of Saturday 23 September carried a picture of Stillwell leaving the court, albeit with a raincoat covering his face, on its front page. Their stance was firmly in the camp that the magistrates had reached the correct decision:

> There was a celebration dinner at a Chichester hotel last night for Tom Stillwell, the tow-headed decorator, who spent two years under suspicion of murder because he went poaching.
>
> Last night he vowed to keep for ever the white heather given him for luck by his fiancée. He wore it throughout the hearing.
>
> For although life started anew last night for Stillwell, he will keep the heather in case fate forges around him another circumstantial chain like the one which snapped among cheering at 2.17 p.m. yesterday.

The following day the *Sunday Chronicle* revealed that Thomas Stillwell had been out shopping in Guildford the previous day and was relishing his resumed liberty. They claimed that the women of Arundel were now walking in fear – of the real murderer still being loose. They quoted a Mrs Sybil Cook of High Street, Arundel, mother of two children, as saying: 'Until the killer is found we can never be really easy in our minds around here. We have known young Tom Stillwell since he was a baby, and we are glad he is free.'

Meanwhile, Thomas Jacks soon received a very different message from the 'women of Arundel'. The letter he received, postmarked Arundel, is reproduced below:

Arundel

Sussex

29/9/50

To Mr Jacks

Dear Sir

We thought you would just like to know that if 50 magistrates discharged Stillwell almost everybody in Arundel and Littlehampton would still have there [*sic*] way, and say, that he is guilty of murder. He is nothing more or less than a dirty swine, and should have been put in prison years ago for accosting women and young girls in the park or anywhere else.

We know of a case of a young girl that was walking along the river bank at Arundel and there was nobody in sight and then all of a sudden Tom Stillwell appeared in front of her, from behind some bushes; he almost frightened her to death and was going to throw her in the river if he could not have his own way.

We are writing just to let you know what a filthy beast he is. It would not matter who the girl was he would walk alongside of her and she could not get rid of him, so we do hope the people that read the papers about Joan Woodhouse will know that she was not walking along with him, he was accosting her, like he do all females that he catches alone, and there is some people in Arundel that can read him like a book, he know where Joan was and he was stalking her like a bird do its prey.

Everybody's allowed to have an opinion and he is such a filthy beast that we think that the hair that was found on Joan he came back 2 or 3 days after he had killed her and put that there so as the 'tecs' should think it was somebody else, because he is as cunning as a fox, and we also think he went back to the body and folded up her clothes and we do not think for one moment that she was lying in the copse, she may have been right near, and he caught her unawares, and almost strangled her, and carried her in the copse, and that was why we think her arms were not scratched, and we do not believe that she took any of her clothes off herself.

Stillwell did that, the dirty beast; and did his mother wash his clothes? People are saying that he went back to the body several times before he reported it to the police.

We are sorry to write to you, but we had to have our opinion because almost everybody in Arundel knows what a swine Stillwell is.

You got the right man Mr Jacks, for nobody else but Stillwell killed Joan Woodhouse.

We will tell you another thing he will do. He will wait to the last buses or trains have run into Arundel and hide somewhere and then if there is a young girl walking alone he will accost her, and she will not get rid of him and tell him you will phone the police about him, he would not go away. And he will also go to Arundel Park and expose himself to little children, in fact no female is safe along a country lane, or in the park if there is no other people about.

Will you tell Mr Woodhouse, Joan's Dad, that you did get the right man, Tom Stillwell is guilty of murdering his Joan.

Well Mr Jacks, hope you do not mind us writing to you.

There are fifteen people here while I am writing this letter and we are so sore about it, and we do feel sorry for Joan's Dad and two Aunties, and will you tell them we say a little prayer for them every night and that the murder shall be brought to book, TOM STILLWELL.

We are not signing our names, there are 15 altogether round the table helping to write this to you Mr Jacks.

So now we all 15 say 'Good luck, Mr Jacks, you had your man, (Tom Stillwell)'

PS We think it is a waste of time looking for anyone else.

x x x x x x x x x x x x x x x

Signed 15 people of Arundel

Although this was one of several anonymous letters received by the private detective – and many more had been sent to the local police and newspapers – Jacks was sufficiently convinced of its veracity to submit it to the DPP and the police. John Woodhouse and the aunts saw it as further vindication of their pursuit of Stillwell.

Reading the letter now its language and style do suggest the hand of a local woman or women or someone that has cleverly disguised themselves as such. The term 'filthy beast' would suggest a female description rather than a man's, and knowledge of Stillwell's habit of exposing himself to young girls, and the river incident (which was never aired in court) and the claim of him waiting for buses to accost females point to local knowledge of the man as well as information not in the public domain.

Conversely, however, Stillwell's camp could have argued that the letter actually *supports* his innocence. They could contend that the letter was written by the real murderer or somebody protecting the real murderer in an attempt to keep the heat on Stillwell and prevent the authorities reopening the case and searching elsewhere. The PS – 'We think it is a waste of time looking for anyone else' – could be interpreted in this way, and the notion of fifteen village women gathered around a table in a room somewhere jointly putting together this anonymous letter could, in the cold light of day, appear far-fetched.

Whoever did write the letter raised an interesting theory on how Joan met her death. Was it possible that Joan never entered a remote area of Box Copse, removed her clothes and sunbathed? Did the murderer accost her as she walked nearby? Did he stun her and pull her into the copse or chase her there? Did he assault, rape and strangle her and at his leisure remove her clothes, fold them and generally interfere with the murder scene? If he had been revisiting the body between the time of the murder and the 'discovery' of the body, he would indeed have had ample opportunity to undress Joan, fold her clothes and even place foreign hairs on her person. He may have confided in his mother, and she, as some local people gossiped and speculated, may have guided him in this direction, finally advising him to 'find' the corpse. Perhaps the pressure of knowing it was lying there waiting to be found was too much for Stillwell to bear.

On the other hand, in the week between the murder and the discovery of Joan's body nobody reported any significant changes in Tom's behaviour or outward signs of being stressed. He went about his business as usual – for example, playing darts at the Black Rabbit on the day he reported his macabre find. If he were as cunning as Fred Narborough, Thomas Jacks and the Woodhouse family and friends all believed, why didn't he leave well alone and leave Joan's body to decompose and disappear or wait for some other poor soul to stumble upon it?

20
SUNDAY SCOOPS

The *News of the World*, predictably, was the only newspaper to refer to some parts of the committal-hearing evidence that the other newspapers chose to ignore or suppress. Perhaps they were indignant at their rival the *Sunday Dispatch* having scooped Stillwell's personal exclusive. It was probably because of this exclusive with the *Dispatch* that Stillwell covered his head with a raincoat when *leaving* the court as an innocent man. Most people when cleared of a crime, or as good as, like to emerge from court head held high.

The *NOTW* mentioned Stillwell's statement when he had admitted that he was in the park on the favoured day of the murder with the intention of acting 'improperly' in front of two small girls and that he had followed and tried to catch up the girl he believed to be Joan Woodhouse. This was the only public mention of Stillwell's sexual perversion and criminal activity outside of the court and police interview rooms until Reginald Spooner's biography, *The Great Detective*, was released in 1966. Here, again, Spooner alludes to the statement and of Stillwell's confessed intention to indecently expose himself to two small girls on the day of discovering the body.

The *Sunday Dispatch*, owned by Lord Rothermere, was at its peak and boasted more than two million readers. Once their issue of 24 September 1950 hit the newsstands it was apparent why Tom Stillwell had been so reticent on leaving court a few days before. He had sold his story to them and only them. It dominated the front page, pushing American planes bombing British troops in Korea and a gasworkers' strike to the margins and followed up inside with a two-page splash and promises of more the following week. It is the only public statement made by Stillwell himself, and as such is worth reproducing in full. Even though the cleared man would have had the assistance of a ghostwriter it is one of the few opportunities we have to hear Stillwell's true voice.

WHAT HAPPENED
By Thomas Stillwell

This is my story. I have made no statement of any kind to any other newspaper – verbal or otherwise – since my arrest.

Have you ever had a nightmare in which you were standing on the edge of a high cliff? You were looking down a precipice and felt you were about to fall.

At that instant, when the terror of hurtling down gripped you, you woke up, sweating, trembling, wondering.

That was what I felt on Friday when after the lunch interval in Arundel Court, the five magistrates filed in and the chairman, Mr West, announced that I was a free man.

My nightmare has lasted more than two years. For it began very soon after I found the body of Joan Woodhouse in Box Copse in Arundel Park on August 10, 1948.

No Easy Ride

At first sight I did not know that it was a dead body. It took a second closer look to tell me that. I stood like a statue for . . . how long I cannot say. It may have been seconds. It may have been a minute or more. And then I made for Swanbourne Lake Lodge, for the house of Mr Ferris, one of the Duke's keepers.

I told him: 'There is the body of a woman in Box Copse. I am going in to Arundel police to tell them about it. Can you lend me a bike?' He gave me his daughter's. With my arm in a sling, because of a poisoned finger, and with brakes that were none too good, it was no easy ride but I made it.

The police, a sergeant and a constable, set out right away and I followed. I rode the bike back to Box Copse, but I could not bring myself to look on that dead body again.

On the road near the lodge I ran into my mother as she was walking home to our cottage at Offham, and told her about my discovery. Then later I went home to tea and after that to the Black Rabbit pub, where I played darts.

Police Found It

It was then that I missed one of my three darts and wondered where I'd lost it. It must, I thought, have fallen from my jacket pocket that day when I was gardening. I looked for it where I'd been, but did not find it.

Later in the week I happened to ask the police if they had seen it anywhere and they told me they had found it at Box Copse. Presumably it had fallen from my jacket pocket when I had bent down in the first place to examine the clothing.

I am not vindictive, I hope, but I have to say bluntly that it did not take long for me to become aware that tongues were wagging, and in a place the size of Arundel, where I was born 26 years ago and where I have lived every day of my life except for a brief time working on jobs during the war, when one tongue begins to wag there are many ears eager to listen.

The people knew me first as a butcher's boy, delivering meat to their houses when I was 14.

Knew Park

They knew me as a jobbing gardener, tending their lawns and flower-beds. They have known me as a builder and painter, going to work on my bike.

I believe the first indication I got of how gossip, malicious and slandering, had begun was when one of my mates at work said one morning: 'I bet you won't go finding any more dead bodies, Tom.'

I asked him what he meant. He had, it is true, said it in an attempt at joking. But he was serious enough when he answered: 'Haven't you heard what folks are saying?'

I said I had heard nothing. He shrugged his shoulders and muttered something like: 'They say you had something to do with that girl's death.'

It was bad enough for me to hear that. But then my mother, standing in bus queues, and going about her rounds for the family, began to hear my name mentioned. Always it was coupled with the name of Joan Woodhouse. Many of the people did not know my mother by sight, and often they talked openly, saying: 'Of course, we know very well who murdered the girl.' My name inevitably followed.

In Littlehampton, in Worthing, everywhere I went, I now got accustomed, if I may put it that way – to seeing heads turn, sometimes fingers pointing at me, and hands going to mouths to cover remarks. There came a day when I was sacked from my job of painting. I was told I was working too slowly. But I wondered then. And I wonder now.

I did not know then, but hardly a day passed without anonymous letters arriving at our home addressed to me. They were all in the same terms.

They accused me of having murdered Joan Woodhouse; they called me everything that abuse could think of. Some of them threatened my life.

My mother snatched them from the postman and never let me see any of them. Nor did she tell me until a long time later that they had arrived.

She handed them over, most of them, to my uncle, Mr Parsons. He too kept silent so far as I was concerned.

Now when I was a butcher's boy, delivering goods at the house of a gamekeeper and his wife, I met their daughter. She was 11.

We did not, of course, walk out; she was very shy. But it was to develop into courtship years later and we became engaged last Christmas.

My fiancée too began to receive anonymous letters – even after she and her mother had moved to Horsham, which showed how well the writers knew her movements.

Her Ordeal

One day, at their house, my fiancée's mother let drop that anonymous letters had arrived there and realised I knew nothing about them. I saw what a terrible ordeal my fiancée was going through, and my mother as well.

I want to make one thing clear. I did not know Joan Woodhouse. To the best of my knowledge I had never met her in my life, either at Arundel or anywhere else.

Many people who have read the details of this baffling affair may have got the idea that Miss Woodhouse, who, it seems, left her hostel in London to go to her home in Yorkshire but somehow journeyed down to Arundel instead, may have made that trip to keep some other appointment, secret or otherwise.

Well, if she did, it was not with me. As I have said, I had not the slightest knowledge of her existence.

There came the time when the police seemed to become busy on their inquiries into the murder of Joan Woodhouse. Murder it was. Having attended the inquest, I know very well that that was so.

One of the jury in the coroner's court asked a question about me. 'Why,' he said 'is this man Stillwell represented by a solicitor?'

Uncle's Advice

I can answer that question now. I shall do so as I was still on oath. My uncle,

Mr Parsons, knew, and realised very well, that my position was, to say the least, very awkward. I mean in a legal sense.

Now, may I say I am no chawbacon. But at the same time I know nothing of the law. Nor do I want to from now on. So, when Uncle Bill Parsons advised me to be represented, I took his advice, and Mr Vincent Jackson was in court.

After that the nightmare became more and more lurid; more swift; more like some cinema operator who has lost control of his projector and shows on the screen some picture upside down, backways, foremost, blurred as sand raised by a whirlwind.

There was Narborough from the Yard, West Sussex CID. I have no grudge against them. They had a job to do. They were fair to me, all of them. I hope they realise I was fair to them.

Enter Mr Jacks

Then one day I was told that a Mr Jacks had arrived in Arundel. I heard that he had been employed by the aunt of Joan Woodhouse to take up the case 'where the Yard had left it off'. Take it from me – and who should know better – the Yard never left it off.

I understand that Mr Jacks said sometime, somewhere, that 'he had spoken to the guilty man'. That is OK by me. For, I was not the guilty man. I can only add that, whoever that 'guilty man' was, it certainly was not myself. For at no time has Mr Jacks ever talked to me, or with me.

Through all of this my wife-to-be remained loyal, true in every sense of the word.

Then there came Spooner, again 'from the Yard'. I want to say here that, like the other CID men that saw me, questioned me, tried to twist me in a perfectly legitimate way – for it was their job – Mr Spooner was what I can only describe as an absolute gentleman. But that did not lessen my nightmare.

For, while I was at work I didn't know from one moment to the next when the foreman would come to me and say: 'You are wanted by police officers, who'd like to ask some more questions.'

I have only one complaint to make about the part the police played in this two-year nightmare of mine. They went once to our little cottage where I was born and in my absence went right through my room, searched the dressing table drawers, and my mother, bless her, did not know enough to query that action and ask if they had a search warrant.

Gave Up Job

To be perfectly candid, neither would I have known if I had been there. For, as I have said, I know nothing about law or police powers.

Meanwhile, my fiancée had to give up her job in Arundel as an assistant in a drapery store. Loose talk, gossip, was becoming too strong. Because everyone knew that she and I had become engaged, she was linked up with me, the suspect. And when she and I met, went to the cinema or elsewhere, her comment on peoples' remarks was: 'Tom, they must be mad.'

I had received a letter from Mrs Sheriff – one of Joan Woodhouse's aunts in Bridlington – asking me if she and her sister came to Arundel, 'would I go with them to the spot where I had found the body'.

I wrote back in answer, and said I certainly would. I told her she and the other aunt would be welcome to come at any time to our cottage, and though we have not a lot of room, Arthur, my brother, and I would be prepared to 'sleep rough', and they could stay with my parents at the cottage. I got no reply to that.

No Evidence

Again, after that, Mr Jacks came back to Arundel. I knew he was making inquiries all round. I can only say about that I am glad he was so thorough, now that the nightmare has ended. For those inquiries only confirmed what the Scotland Yard men had found. There was no evidence whatsoever that I was the 'guilty man'.

I shall tell you next week of the last phase of my nightmare. How, at long last, the blow came in the shape of me being arrested.

Did I say blow?

Can you understand me when I say it came as a relief? For, from the moment I walked up from the cottage between Detective Inspector Dean and Sergeant Cowley to be taken to Arundel Police Station, charged with murder, and then to Littlehampton, I felt: This is a crisis. But it will at least end my nightmare.

Despite Stillwell's assurance that he had not spoken to any other newspapers the *Sunday Pictorial* had him talking directly to them on their front page and also inside. To underline the authenticity they even reproduced his signature.

Again, Stillwell complains about the gossipmongers and the pressure this had brought to bear on his family, especially his mother. He beseeches the police to find the real killer and declares that would be the best wedding present he could ever receive. The paper itself was moved to carry the following editorial:

On page 1 today we print a photograph of Thomas Stillwell, of Arundel, the most discussed man in Britain. Look at the picture – read Stillwell's own story below – and then forget about them both.

For Stillwell must no longer be a man apart, a man to be spied upon and whispered about.

The *Pictorial* is glad that a private citizen was able to bring a warrant against Stillwell when the police decided they could not charge him with the murder of Joan Woodhouse. We are glad, too, that after a lengthy hearing the Arundel magistrates decided there was no case for him to answer.

Stillwell's story is the story of a man who went through two years of mental anguish – an anguish shared by his family and the girl he loves.

PERHAPS NOW THE UGLY SPECTACLE OF GOSSIP, SUSPICION AND WHISPERED RUMOURS WILL CEASE IN THE LITTLE VILLAGES AROUND ARUNDEL. PERHAPS NOW TOM STILLWELL WILL BE AT LAST ALLOWED TO LIVE HIS LIFE IN PEACE.

If that leader did not appal those who felt Stillwell to be far from an innocent victim of circumstance, the second part of his *Sunday Dispatch* feature, published on 1 October 1950, would.

The Girl In The Park
By Thomas Stillwell

What of the girl I did meet in Arundel Park?

I use the word 'meet' in a very broad sense. If by meeting her one means anything arranged beforehand, any conversations with each other as between friends or acquaintances, I never did meet any girl. What happened was a simple chance encounter – not at all unusual in Arundel Park or similar places – that lasted no more than a few seconds.

Here is exactly what happened.

I was walking along that day from the direction of the lake towards the big walnut tree. Ahead of me was a girl walking. I then spotted Phil Challen and Frank Clements (both of whom gave evidence at the police court hearing) and with them was Challen's little daughter going the same way.

As I caught up with them I saw the little girl had a bumble bee caught in her butterfly net. She was frightened of getting stung, and I ran over with the idea of releasing the bee from the net. Before I got there, however, the child herself lifted the net and the bee flew away. I then said something to Challen and Clements. I know I mentioned that the chances of getting many walnuts later were pretty poor as we were near the walnut tree.

It was after I had passed another remark or two that I saw the girl I had first seen taking the path to the right. It leads to Dry Lodge – a wood on the highest part of the park. Challen and Clements and the girl Challen moved on in the same direction as the girl ahead. I sat down near the walnut tree and after a few minutes got up and walked up the slope to Box Copse.

Challen and Clements had by then gone about 250 to 300 yards and turned off the pathway up the slope in a direction that would lead them to the open ground at the top of Box Copse. The girl was still walking up towards Dry Lodge. As I watched her she turned around and began to walk towards me. I then walked towards her and passed her near the end of the trees round which Challen and Clements had now gone.

The girl was wearing a full-fitting coat of some dark material. She seemed to me about medium build, but owing to the full coat it was difficult to tell exactly.

As I passed her I gave her the time of day. I can't remember the exact words I used to greet her. Something like 'Good morning' or 'Good afternoon'. Anyhow, she just looked at me for a moment and went on her way without answering me at all.

I went up to the left-hand slope and sat down. From that point I noticed a group of Girl Guides sitting on the opposite slope some distance farther along towards where Challen and Clements had gone up the bank.

I might tell you I am not a great walker since I broke my ankle playing football for the Arundel team I helped to start. My leg still makes me walk a bit lame.

As I sat there I lost sight of the girl altogether. I got up and walked towards Target Bottom. Then I saw the girl once more near the walnut tree, where she turned to her left and went towards the lake. As I watched her she passed right out of sight along the path and around the bend.

That was the last I ever saw of her. I cannot say for certain that I would know her again if I met her. What I do feel sure about – as far as one can be sure in the case of seeing a strange girl passing for moment without much chance of studying her features – and then some time later coming across a dead girl's body – is that the girl was not Joan Woodhouse.

Nor can I remember the day of the week the encounter happened, or whether it was morning or afternoon. There was nothing special about that chance meeting. It is the sort of thing that can happen to anyone who, like myself, strolls in Arundel Park. Let anyone who reads what I am writing ask himself or herself: 'Could I say for certain where I was at such and such a time on a day weeks ago unless, perhaps, there was some very special incident to bring it to the memory?'

My nightmare has ended. So now it is the present and the future, and not the past, I have to think about. Especially the future.

No easy problem when you realise, as I do full well, that you have been going about for two years and more in a small country town – where everyone knows everyone else – and have been a suspect; where my home and my family are: where my work lies.

I lay at nights – and days too – in Brixton Jail thinking hard about that problem. Many people, people whom I know to be good friends, have said to me: 'Tom, why, when this is all over, don't you get right out of the district? Start fresh somewhere you aren't known.'

Why should I? Why should I run away like a coward because all this happened to me and made me the most-talked-of man in the country, the man who has been the centre of what I now realise is the only one of its exact kind in the history of law in England?

There is, too, another person beside myself whom I have to think about in deciding my future – my intended, 23 years of age, an invalid for many years when she was a child and none too strong in health now. Every day, there in Brixton Jail, the cell door would open in the morning and a prison officer would hand me two letters – one from my mother and one from my fiancée.

They made the nightmare bearable. I have them in my pocket now. I shall keep them all my life. Neither she nor my mother have any pretence at being great letter writers. Nothing flowery; no attempt at fine-sounding phrases. We are just simple folk down West Sussex way with no notions of being 'bookish'.

But the greatest love letters that have ever been written by people who write fine English have never had half the meaning of those my fiancée has written me daily. For they were sincere, deep, warm; they told me in every one of them that although I had been accused of the most horrible crime imaginable, not for one moment would she ever dream of taking off the modest little engagement ring I had put on her finger last year; nor for a moment would she hesitate to marry me and live anywhere I chose.

We got to know each other well first through trouble.

A very different kind of trouble from the one I have just finished with. The trouble of illness that led to her father's death at their home just outside Arundel.

I first saw her when I was a butcher's boy delivering at their house. It was a good many years later that my mother got to know her parents and they occasionally visited each other. The father had an incurable disease and towards the end of his life was in awful pain most of the time.

My intended and her mother took it in turns to nurse him and that meant that they both lost a lot of sleep. For her especially that was serious because one of her lungs was not too good. I forget whether it was my mother or myself who suggested it. But we fixed up to take it in turns to go over to the house and sit up all night so that she and her mother could get a full night's rest.

Neither my mother nor I have ever thought we were doing anything very special. I know neither of us would ever think of it to take any credit for having done that till the father died. It was just one of those things we folk in the country do. I think in places like where I have lived all my life, in cottages sometimes a long way from the next neighbour, we are more sympathetic maybe than town folk. You get that way.

So you see it was then that we fell in love. The love that began in the bond of trouble and increased through the trouble that ended in her father's death, was to go on getting greater through still more trouble – this matter of my being arrested as the result of a private application after two Scotland Yard experts and the experienced CID men of West Sussex had advised there was no evidence to warrant that.

Well, I have at any rate for the moment decided to go back home. I feel I owe that to my mother, whose birthday I could not attend last week because of the case. I feel I owe to it my fiancée. And I feel I owe it to myself.

I have only one ambition. It is nothing very high. Just to be able with my hands or my head or both to earn a wage that will enable me to marry my loved one, to settle down with her if need be in as simple a little cottage as my parents' at Offham. For I know she would be content with that.

I have two trades I can follow – painting and building. I know more than a little too about the manufacture of tar macadam and road laying material, for that was the last job I was on at the time they arrested me.

It seems to me that for a long time to come anyway there should be plenty of employment in those trades. I know my fiancée would be willing to take some kind of job to help make the money more [sic] for us both. She has told me so since I walked out of Arundel Court and eventually managed to see her with her mother. But I would not want that if we can avoid it because my main thought is for her to get really strong and well. In fact I want her job to be being my wife and – who knows – maybe one day mother of my children.

I know it may all be difficult. Perhaps employers might shy at having me. But for the present, at any rate. I am all right that way because the firm I was with at the time of my arrest told me that they would be quite willing to have me back as soon as I was a free man again.

Do not think all the people down Arundel way – or anywhere else – have been malignant gossipmongers, or that all of the letters, anonymous or with names and addresses, have been abusive or against me.

I have had many, many friendly ones, sympathetic ones, offers to help me in whatever small way they could. I had packets of cigarettes sent to Brixton which were quite ample to ensure I did not want for a smoke. And how one does want for a smoke lying around all day in a prison cell. The food they gave me was excellent. As for drink, I do not use it. I have been a teetotaller for many years, and then I only had an odd mild-and-bitter when I was about 21 or 22 but gave it up because I could not afford it.

Yes, I am a teetotal darts player who visits pubs and plays on an orange squash or two.

Now a thing quite a few people have asked me is: Shall I ever help the police again if circumstances arose where I could? I can tell you that once or twice I have asked myself the same question.

But I can give the answer now. Yes, certainly, and with no qualifications attached to it. I would always help the police if I found myself in a position where I could do so.

I do not have to say that I hope there never will in my life again be such circumstances; certainly not such as might lead to my finding a dead body whether of a man or a woman. That day in Arundel Park when I did so, when I never hesitated to get a bike and ride in to the police station as quickly as possible, is quite sufficient for one lifetime.

But I say again that even if it involved trouble of any kind I would help the police, either in Sussex or anywhere else it might be. In any case, I have no grudge against the police. They did their job, and that was that so far as I am concerned. I would reckon myself a pretty poor kind of citizen if, because of what happened to me, I nursed a grouch and refused to give assistance if the police wanted it.

Stillwell's impertinence and contempt, as they saw it, sent the aunts apoplectic with rage. On the 12 October 1950 they wrote to Inspector Spooner and he got a piece of their mind. They asked him why he had said 'We are with you all the way' when he clearly did not mean it. They referred to a 'family party' of Establishment members who all knew their role. It was a bitter but heartfelt letter concluding that 'face-saving and prestige' had been permitted to override British justice.

In another letter to Spooner Lena Bamber alleges that Inspector Narborough had been forcibly retired on a reduced pension because of his incompetence in this inquiry and Spooner had confirmed this. There are no replies on the family files from Spooner denying the statement.

A few days later the family received a letter from Christopher Soames, the newly elected Conservative MP for Bedford and son-in-law of wartime leader Winston Churchill. It is not clear why he was contacted, but all he could offer was sympathy. He claimed there was an unwritten law that one MP should not intervene in the affairs of another member's constituents.

Joan's aunts would have been further disheartened to read an opinion column in their local paper, the *Hull Daily Mail* of 28 October 1950 which was reacting to a news story about the fund that had been opened in Hull to attract donations to help fight the case:

> Some funds attract immediate public sympathy, but it is hardly likely that the one which has been opened in Hull in connection with the Arundel Murder Case will come within that category.
>
> Scotland Yard have made a patient and careful investigation of the facts and the jury have given their verdict. In these circumstances it is difficult to avoid the conclusion that fund is a misguided adventure.

Mr Dickinson, the solicitor, was appalled by this attempt to quell the fund before it had even been properly launched and was baffled by the newspaper's stance. He protested strongly, pointing out that no jury had ever delivered a verdict in this case and that it had never got to go in front of a criminal trial jury *at all* – that was the injustice being fought. But there is no surviving evidence of a retraction from the newspaper.

A fresh low point for the family was reached days after these articles appeared when the attorney general, Hartley Shawcross, railed against private prosecutions generally in Parliament and referred to the Arundel case and made the comment in the House of Commons that the Woodhouse family had 'persecuted' their suspect. John Woodhouse was moved to write to Shawcross on 4 November 1950:

> When an Attorney General uses the privilege of his position to infer the family's efforts to obtain justice are 'persecution' one wonders whether justice still exists in this country. Persecution, yes, to the full, but of the family of the innocent victim. We complained of this 'sting of persecution' in 1948.
>
> My God, Sir, I only wish you could know and suffer the same loss and persecution, then only could you understand how our fight has been the only means of saving our sanity.

John Woodhouse's sanity would have been severely tested by the attorney general's reply:

From Hartley Shawcross
Attorney General
8 November 1950

Dear Mr Woodhouse,

Thank you for your letter. I want you to know I do realise very fully the bitter distress that you feel in regard to the murder of your daughter and the fact that it is impossible to bring anyone to justice on account of her murder. I am afraid, however, that you have not appreciated the high degree of proof which is required in order to establish a capital charge, or that the evidence in this case falls short of what is necessary. You really must try to get it out of your mind that there has been any desire on the part of the authorities to shelve the case or to do anything other than to discover adequate evidence on which to base a persecution [*sic*].

Yours sincerely

Hartley Shawcross

How crushed John Woodhouse must have been when he received this letter, the attorney general's Freudian slip revealing his true feelings about the case. Mr Woodhouse knew he meant to write *prosecution* and was too polite to point this out in his reply, or, perhaps, he had by this time simply given up.

21
JUSTICE FOR JOAN

In the blaze of all this publicity Joan's aunts had retreated to Lena Bamber's home in Derbyshire to avoid intrusive press interest, at least for a few days. They issued a statement saying that, as far as they were concerned, the hunt for Joan's killer would continue and settled down to writing more angry, pleading and conscience-pricking letters to the great and the good of the land.

Deep inside they knew that the justice they had already felt was slipping away from their grasp was now firmly adrift. Their letters to all and sundry transmitted their personal misery, despair and crushed spirits over the legal process, while Mr Dickinson, their solicitor, addressed the legal process itself. Theobald Mathew, the DPP, and James Chuter Ede, the home secretary, were key recipients, although Mr Bass, the prosecution counsel, and *his* conscience, remained a target of the redoubtable aunts.

Mr James Chuter Ede was a Unitarian Christian, a deeply religious man who had himself come up against Establishment cover-ups thirty years earlier, long before he became a part of the government machine.

In 1919, as a very young politician in his home town of Epsom, Surrey, he served as foreman on the inquest into the death of a homely police-sergeant at the hands of Canadian soldiers. Sergeant Thomas Green was the first mainland policeman to die in a civil riot in the twentieth century. (It was more than sixty years later that PC Blakelock became the tragic second at Broadwater Farm, Tottenham, London, in 1985.) The Canadian soldiers were hospitalised in the town, having been removed from the front line during the First World War and, by 1919 were immensely frustrated about still not having been transported home. Frustrations exploded one summer's evening, which resulted in the battering of Sergeant Green as he and other policeman tried to prevent rioters entering the country police station and freeing two of their men being held there. However, Secretary of State for War Winston Churchill and Prime Minister David Lloyd George, while appalled at Thomas' death, were keen that nobody should singly stand trial for the murder and, more importantly, be publicly executed.

The Canadian nation had sacrificed much for the mother country in the war and relations were strained. There was talk of withdrawing from the Empire. The notion of hanging Canadian soldiers sent shivers down the government's spine. They were prepared to sacrifice justice, even for a murdered policeman, in the cause of high-level international diplomacy.

The legal process was therefore manipulated from the beginning to achieve a mutually acceptable result, and James Chuter Ede, in his capacity as inquest jury foreman, was an early barrier for the Establishment to overcome as he picked holes in the cursory police investigation and innocently tried to ensure possible suspects were not allowed to return home before standing trial. His decency and empathy was demonstrated by a local paper reporting how, on the first day of the inquest, he had picked a rose and placed it on the dead body of Sergeant Green.

However, thirty years later he was deaf to the Woodhouse family's entreaties. By that time he was a seasoned minister, statesman and career politician, who was accustomed to seeing a bigger picture.

Ida and Annie complained in particular about the evidence relating to the hair on the brassière being introduced at the last minute and without the knowledge of the prosecution, therefore depriving them of the ability to cross-examine. If this evidence had been available in 1948, how was it this was the first time that this crucial finding had been mentioned? They made it clear that they smelled a rat.

Their letters accused Scotland Yard of blundering, too, especially in relation to not recovering and examining Thomas Stillwell's boots, which they believed would have held traces of bark from the tree that had been damaged in whatever struggle it was that Joan Woodhouse had endured. They also referred to their belief that there was a strong difference in opinion between West Sussex CID and Scotland Yard over Stillwell's culpability.

Mr Dickinson wrote formally to the DPP about the 'new' pubic-hair evidence on 20 October 1950:

According to the witness, Holden, the pubic hair was in his possession on the 12 August 1948. No mention was made to me by the Director at my interview with him. Stillwell was questioned by the police on 7 September 1948 and again on the 19 October. Why was not an examination of Stillwell made on either of these two dates and why wait until 15 September 1950? The witness, Keith Simpson, who saw the body in the park on the 11 August 1948 never saw any signs of pubic hair on the brassière. The deceased was living in a room in a hostel occupied by two other girls, but they were never examined.

John Woodhouse was also firing off correspondence in his anger and despair. His letter to the DPP suggests that he, even more than his sisters-in-law, knew that the end of the road was in sight. He signed off with: 'May God forgive you and all those responsible for this wicked travesty of justice.'

He particularly felt that the weight of Frederick Chamberlain's evidence had not been sufficiently recognised. Here was a man, Stillwell, wrote John Woodhouse, who had said he was cycling furiously to the police station, distressed, to report the discovery of a dead body yet he stops and chats to the publican of his local inn. The first topic of conversation was *not* the grisly, highly upsetting discovery of a dead body supposedly minutes earlier but Stillwell's bandaged hand. Stillwell then says that this is the least of his troubles and mentions the body – saying it was woman of about twenty-six and twenty-seven years of age. How could he have possibly known that when the face was unrecognisable?

Also the duty sergeant said Stillwell was in an excited state when he entered the police station, commensurate with someone who had just stumbled on a dead body. Yet, seconds earlier, he had been chatting calmly with Frederick Chamberlain. Joan's father saw this as evidence of the cunning character of the accused man.

Mr Dickinson, the solicitor, summed up in his letter to the DPP:

To say that my clients are disappointed and disgusted with the conduct of your nominee is to put it mildly. The opening speech was the clearest invitation to the magistrates to decline to the send the case to trial. No attempt was ever made to re-examine the witnesses as the case was conducted with little or no enthusiasm.

I am now instructed to inform you that the whole of the facts will be placed before Mr Arthur S. Moody [MP for Gateshead] so that the matter can be raised in the House of Commons by questions to the Home Secretary and the learned Attorney General [Sir Hartley Shawcross].

Mr Dickinson expanded on this, telling the *Yorkshire Evening Press* that the aim was to get an amendment to the Act that allows the DPP to conduct all prosecutions in which the death penalty was involved when the warrant was issued on a private application. He said, 'The family's solicitor ought to be allowed to present the case and engage his own counsel. All I had was a watching brief and could not say anything. My complaint is that the Director invited the examining magistrates not to commit for trial.'

Arthur Seymour Moody was a joiner and had been active in the Amalgamated Society of Woodworkers before being elected to Parliament as a Labour Party MP in the 1945 general election, which saw a large swing towards Labour. Prior to this the local man, born in 1891, had served on Hull City Council. It was natural, therefore, for Ida Sheriff, Annie Blades, Thomas Jacks and Mr Dickinson to approach him, but as buccaneering MPs go he may not have been the best choice.

He was a very quiet parliamentarian with little in the way of gravitas. He rarely asked questions in the House throughout his career. Years later, in 1963, he was lampooned by the satirical TV show *That Was The Week That Was* for not having made a single speech in the House of Commons since the previous election. His only real incursion into the national press was in 1948 when he had broken the whip to oppose an annuity to be paid to the future Queen Elizabeth and the Duke of Edinburgh after their marriage.

At the same time the family also revealed that they had decided to apply for a bill of indictment against Stillwell to be heard at Sussex Assizes on 6 December 1950 in front of Mr Justice Humphreys. Mr Dickinson told the press: 'It is necessary in preferring a bill of indictment to present fresh information. The judge has the power to ask for witnesses and order a trial.'

To embolden their case the family instructed Hector Hughes, KC, to provide counsel's opinion. Hughes was a maverick barrister with a colourful history. He was born in 1887 in Dublin and was called to the bar there in 1915, and he would later take silks at the English and Irish bars. He had been a passionate supporter of the Irish labour movement and had helped organise the Irish General Strike of 1913. In England he became involved in politics, too, joining the Fabian Society. After two unsuccessful attempts at getting himself elected to Parliament he became the MP for Aberdeen North, a seat he held until his retirement in 1970 at the good age of eighty-three. An obituary in *The Times* said that, although he was short of stature and somewhat pugnacious in manner at times, he was the warmest-hearted of men, having a host of friends and few enemies. The obituarist also noted he had deep religious convictions and was for a long time on the board of the Church Army and had taken an active part in the Salvation Army. Finally it was recorded that Hector Hughes was a strong believer in physical fitness, and was particularly fond of swimming. 'No matter what the weather he enjoyed a dip in the sea at Aberdeen at any time of the year, and took part in the Christmas Day race at Highgate Pond, London,' said *The Times*.

It was this fondness for natural swimming that proved to be his undoing. His political rivals claimed that he only swam publicly to deflect criticism and doubt about his capabilities as a parliamentarian in his advancing years. Whatever his motive, on the 23 June 1970, while swimming off Black Rock, Brighton, Sussex, he got into difficulties, and despite being rescued and being given artificial respiration on the beach he died later in hospital.

A couple of years earlier WH Smith, the bookseller, had prosecuted Hughes for stealing books valued at 93 shillings from their Victoria Station bookstall. He was found guilty and fined £10 with £21 costs. He duly appealed, saying that the taking of the books was an oversight, and was successful. It is likely that this was an aberration on his part, as there was little incentive for him to shoplift because when he died he left an estate valued at £34,784, the equivalent of just over half a million pounds in 2015.

The opinion he provided for the Woodhouse family is reproduced below in full. Because Hughes had the privilege of drawing on Thomas Stillwell's police statements it is the nearest we have to the full text of those statements that were never aired in public.

MISS JOAN MARY WOODHOUSE DECEASED
OPINION

I have carefully considered the copies of depositions and other documents submitted to me for the purpose of advising whether this is a proper case in which to apply for a Bill of Indictment charging Thomas Stillwell with the murder of the late Miss Joan Woodhouse.

The law and procedure are well known to the querist and so it is unnecessary for me to set it out here. If necessary I shall deal with that later.

No one saw the murder alleged. This case rests, therefore, on circumstantial evidence.

Certain circumstantial evidence tending to connect Thomas Stillwell with the murder has, I am informed, been considered by the DPP and has been adduced before Justices who have refused to commit Stillwell on any charge.

In these circumstances it is necessary to examine with care the evidence adduced in order to determine how far that evidence supports any charge against Stillwell.

I shall deal first with the general trend of the evidence and then with particular aspects of it.

The general trend of the evidence as presented places Stillwell under grave suspicion of being the last person to see Joan Woodhouse alive, and of being her murderer. Grave suspicion, however, would not be enough to justify a jury in finding beyond all reasonable doubt that he murdered her.

The matter does not, however, rest there for two reasons:

First, on the evidence available there is at least one new point which is very important and has not yet been taken in this. It arises on the evidence already given by Stillwell as to the injury to his left ankle. It points to the conclusion that Stillwell was the murderer of Joan Woodhouse. I shall elaborate on it further in this opinion.

Secondly, there are left unexplained other important aspects of the case concerning which even now further inquiries should be made, the result of which might tend to resolve either way and beyond reasonable doubt the innocence or guilt of Stillwell.

I am strongly of the opinion, therefore, that the DPP should be invited, with respect, to consider these two aspects of the case before any application is made for leave to prefer a Bill of Indictment.

It would, I think, be convenient to consider the case under the following three headings:

1. The uncontradicted evidence as to the order of events relating to Miss Woodhouse on 31 July 1948.

2.   Propositions which must be established beyond reasonable doubt to justify an application for leave to prefer a Bill of Indictment against Thomas Stillwell and the evidence at present available to establish them including that relating to the new point already referred to.

3.   Unexplained matters which should be investigated.

Consider these three matters in detail:

1.   **The uncontradicted evidence as to the order of events relating to Miss Woodhouse on 31 July 1948.**

Between 9 and 10 a.m. Miss Joan Woodhouse was seen at the YWCA Hostel in London where she lived (per Miss Nicole Ashby). The description of her personal appearance, her attire and a suitcase she carried are available (per Miss Ashby).

Probably between 1 and 1.30 p.m. The suitcase was deposited at Worthing Central Station on 31 July at a time which is not determined but was probably between 1 p.m. and 1.30 p.m (per Sidney George Guess, Jack Fraser and Inspector Alan Hoare).

2 to 2.05 p.m. Mr. R.W. Bowles, Chemist, 28 High Street, Arundel sold a bottle of medicinal Lembar to a young woman whose description resembled that of Miss Woodhouse. An empty Lembar bottle was found beside her body in Box Copse (per Mr Bowles).

2 to 2.30 or 2.45 p.m. Miss Dibley in 39 High Street, Arundel, looked out of the window and saw a young lady (whose description resembled that of Miss Woodhouse) who crossed the High Street from Bus Office to Norfolk Hotel side which is towards Arundel Park and who was walking at leisure towards Arundel Park (per Miss Dibley).

27 minutes later, i.e., 2.32 to 3.12 p.m. It takes a young woman 27 minutes to walk slowly from [the] junction of Mill Road and High Street Arundel to the end of Box Copse (Arundel Park) where the body of Miss Woodhouse was found (per Nancy Hall, police witness).

2.32 or 3.32 p.m. If, therefore, Miss Joan Woodhouse walked slowly at that pace to the Walnut Tree at Box Copse she would have arrived there starting at 2.05 (per Mr Bowles) at 2.32 or 2.45 (per Miss Dibley) at 3.12. Alternatively allowing 20 minutes extra for the stroll by Miss Woodhouse to Dry Lodge and back she would have arrived at Box Copse at approximately either 2.52 p.m or 3.32 p.m.

Between 2 and 4 p.m. when Stillwell left park to catch bus at 3.50 and 4.05 p.m. Stillwell says he was still in Arundel Park.

'I saw a girl . . . about 30 yards in front.'

'I tried to catch this girl up.'

'I had not caught her up by the time I got to the walnut tree where I saw Mr Challen and Mr Clements.'

'I spoke to Clements and Challen.'

'The girl I had been following had then gone up the valley to the right-hand side.'

'Clements and Challen went in the same direction as the girl.'

'I could not see her from the valley but when I climbed the slope at the end of Box Copse I could see her.'

'While I [was] watching she began to walk back the way she had gone.'

'I went towards the pathway she would come down.'

'And passed the girl.'

'When I passed the girl I spoke to her.'

'She ignored me.'

'I whistled after her.'

'I thought to myself "Well, bugger you, then."'

'I wondered where Clements and Challen had gone.'

'I walked up this bank.' (the left-hand bank)

'I could not see Clements and Challen.'

'But I saw a group of Girl Guides.'

'I sat down at the top of the bank and made water.'

'At this time I could not see the girl I had passed.'

'But when I moved further on towards Target Bottom I saw her go round the path towards the end of the lake and pass out of sight around the corner around a steady bend.'

'I walked along the path the same way the girl had gone but I did not see her . . .'

'Walked up the bank where I masturbated' (per Stillwell statement of 7 September 1948).

Before 3.30 p.m. Stillwell left Arundel Park, cycled home, left his cycle

at home, caught either the 3.50 or 4.10 p.m. bus from Arundel to
Littlehampton (per Stillwell).

Between 2.45 and 4 p.m. PF Bragger saw Stillwell cycling towards
Arundel from the direction of his home (per Bragger).

4.05 or 4.20 p.m. Stillwell arrived in Littlehampton. Went to Hepworths and bought a new shirt (per Stillwell).

Between 4.20 and 5.30 p.m. Hepworths sold a shirt of that description
(per Nicklin of Hepworths).

2. **Propositions which must be established beyond reasonable doubt to
   justify an application for leave to prefer a Bill of Indictment against
   Thomas Stillwell are either or both of these:**

   (1) That between 3 and 4 p.m. on 31 July 1948 Miss Joan Woodhouse
       was seen by Stillwell in Arundel Park and followed her into Box
       Copse.
   (2) That between 3 and 4 p.m. on 31 July 1948 Stillwell raped Miss
       Joan Woodhouse in Box Copse. This includes the new point already
       referred to.

As to proposition 2(1) relevant evidence at present available that
Stillwell saw Miss Woodhouse and followed her into the copse is as
follows:

a) Robert Phillip Challen said in chief:
   I remember him saying he was looking for walnuts. The time was
   sometime in the afternoon but I would not say the exact time. I am
   quite sure about that. I saw Stillwell go into Box Copse. I saw him
   enter Box Copse just where the box bushes commence 30 or 40
   yards from the end of the copse. It could have been any time
   between 2 and 4. We (Challen, his daughter aged 6 and Clements)
   walked round the park and came back to Swanbourne Lake from
   the other end of Box Copse.

   In cross-examination he said:

I hadn't been there on the Saturday previous to 31 July 1948. I was working on the Forestry Commission. On the morning of the 31 I was in Angmering painting. I was with Clements in the afternoon.

b) Stillwell statement of 7 September says:

I walked up the slope towards Box Copse. I did not go in the copse, in the direction taken by this girl.

c) Stillwell's statement of 17 October 1948:

... I am now pretty certain I did not go to the park in the morning of Saturday 31 July 1948 as shown in my statement dated 7 September 1948. I know that I was in the park that day and I met Mr Clements and Mr Challen, who had his daughter with him, so it must have been in the afternoon ... As I was walking along the path by the side of the copse I saw a girl walking along the path ahead of me about 30 yards in front. I tried to catch this girl up, but I [had] not caught her up by the time I got to the walnut tree where I saw Mr Challen and Mr Clements and their [sic] daughter ... I spoke to Clements and Challen about the walnut tree and they said it was too early for walnuts as yet but I said, 'If I know they are here I can come and get them,' or words to that effect. I cannot be absolutely certain. The girl I had been following had then gone up the valley to the right-hand side. I went and sat down then by the walnut tree and Clements and Challen went in the same direction taken by the girl. There were some papers I looked at there but I cannot for the life of me remember whether they were papers or letters. I saw Clements and Challen turn off the pathway and go up the slope to the right. At that time I could not see the girl but knew she had gone up the pathway. I then went up the slope towards the corner of Box Copse. On the edge of the bank I turned and saw a girl I had seen previously waving her hand from the slope near Hiorne Tower and I waved back as I thought she was waving to me. Meanwhile, the other girl I had seen was still walking up the path towards Dry Lodge. I couldn't see her from the valley but when I climbed the slope at the end of Box Copse I could see her. I saw the other girl near Hiorne Tower was joined by a man and knew she had not been waving to me. I turned round and noticed the other

165

girl three quarters of the way up the path to Dry Lodge. While I was watching she turned and began to walk back the way she had gone. I went towards the pathway that she would come down, and passed the girl near the end of the trees, that is the group of trees about 150 yards from the walnut tree. When I passed this girl I spoke to her. I said, 'Good afternoon, a lovely day.' Either that or words similar to that. She ignored me and carried on walking without saying anything. I whistled after her but she paid no attention so I thought to myself, 'Well, bugger you, then.' I said it but I don't think she could have heard it as she had gone by. I then wondered where Challen and Clements had gone to and I thought I should be able to see them from the left-hand bank. I wanted to see if they were setting snares or anything. I walked up this bank but I could not see Clements and Challen but I saw a group of Girl Guides sitting against the edge of the Square Plantation. I sat down on top of the bank and made water. I just laid on my side and did that. At this time I could not see the girl I had passed but when I moved further towards Target Bottom, I saw her go round the path towards the end of the lake and pass out of sight around the corner, around a steady bend. I walked down towards the walnut tree in the same direction as the girl but before I had done that I saw a man whom I had seen before on one of the butts in Target Bottom; he was apparently using field glasses. I went along the path the same way the girl had gone but I did not see her when I turned the corner. I walked along towards Arundel Bottom and went up the far bank which is the near bank when you go in. I masturbated behind some bushes and then went back to the Lake entrance . . . She appeared to be 'stand-offish' when I spoke to her – she looked at me and walked down the pathway a bit faster. In my first statement I said that when I found the body I walked into Box Copse because I was taking a short cut home. I have already said that is not true because it was not a short cut. I went there because I was showing myself off or intended to show myself off to two small girls. At the time I was suffering from a weak ankle, in fact I am still suffering from a weak ankle, so I would not climb up the way I told you into Box Copse to make my way home because I know that on the other side of Box Copse the ground is rugged and covered with mole hills. When I had my broken ankle I used to spend a lot of time in the park because I had nothing else to do. I cannot say what time in the afternoon of Saturday 31 July 1948 I went into the park. I know that when I went in I had an appointment at half past three. I know that I left the park in plenty of time to meet the bus because I remember that I waited at Jubilee Gardens by the bridge for the bus to come in. I think I waited there for about 10 minutes before the bus arrived ... Since I haven't had my girl I have wanted to go back to her and I have masturbated myself on these thoughts. I have exposed myself in the park several times since my engagement was broken off and before I met Mary Richardson, but as far as I remember I did not do it when I was with her. Mary used to stay at my house for weekends and sometimes for only a night. We did not sleep together but we spent a lot of time alone. She used to encourage me to have intercourse with her but I never used to 'come off' when I was inside her. I used to withdraw. Most of the time I used to 'come off' before I had ever started to have intercourse with her and then become erect again then I used to put it in again but I had to be careful. She used to tell me that nothing would happen unless we both 'came' together – that was when the danger was. I used to get an erection whilst I was making a fuss of her with my finger in her private part, sometimes she used to hold me but I didn't need much rubbing before I 'came off', it was after that I would get erect and put it in, as soon as I felt I was going to 'come off' I would withdraw when I would 'come off' into a handkerchief as a rule.

d) Frederick Narborough in cross-examination said:
   The change in the statement when he said, 'I am now pretty sure that I did not go in to the park in the morning,' arose from a question by me. I asked him 'Were you in the park in the morning or the afternoon?' I did not mention Clements or Challen I am sure of that.

e) John Pattison said in chief:
   I said, 'Here is a picture of three girls, you say you would know the girl in the park, can you see her here?' I held the photograph out

to him and he looked at it carefully for a minute and said at the picture of Miss Woodhouse: 'I think that's the girl.'

I then said to him: 'You said you would know this girl if you saw her again and I ask you again do you see her here?'

I held the photograph out again and he looked at it and pointed to the picture of the deceased and said: 'Yes, that's the one but she was wearing a dark coat though.'

He then lowered his head and began to cry and said: 'I suppose I'm to blame for what happened to her?'

I said, 'What do you mean by that?' and he replied: 'Well, if that's the girl I saw I expect I frightened her into the copse where she was found.'

Detective Inspector Dean continued to write the statement of the accused but Stillwell interposed and said: 'Mind you, I'm not dead sure it was the girl, but the face and build are the same, that's all I'll put down, it's been worrying me about the girl I spoke to.'

f) According to the narrative as to the order of events the deceased arrived at the walnut tree between 2.32 and 3.12 p.m. Allowing 20 minutes for her stroll towards Dry Lodge and back 2.32 and 3.12 p.m. is on the balance of probabilities the time when Stillwell spoke to her.

From all this evidence it appears that Challen saw Stillwell go into Box Copse between 2 and 4 p.m. Following this Stillwell's evidence is significant. Stillwell admits he followed a girl and he subsequently identified the girl as the deceased; that he climbed the slope towards the corner of Box Copse where he could see her going towards Dry Lodge; that his ankle was still, then, weak. That the girl while he was watching turned and began to come back towards Box Copse; that he went towards the pathway that he knew she must follow; that he spoke to the girl; that he whistled after her; that she ignored him; that he said 'Well, bugger you, then'; that he wondered where Challen and Clements had gone to. Stillwell further admits that he went to the other side of the bank to see where they were. Why? They were in fact walking away from Box Copse. What did Stillwell do then? He knew the girl was near. There is no evidence of any other person near. Stillwell admits that he was sexually excited by the deceased and that after speaking to her he went away and masturbated. In my opinion the circumstantial evidence pointing to the conclusion that Stillwell followed the girl into Box Copse is beyond reasonable doubt, and therefore that proposition 2(1) is established.

As to proposition 2(2) the relevant evidence at present available that Stillwell raped Miss Joan Woodhouse in Box Copse is as follows:

(a)   The evidence at (1) supra.

(b)   The evidence of retired Inspector Narborough who in his statement of 13 August 1948 stated:
'Here we found the body of a woman. It was concealed by its natural surroundings of shrubs high on the side of steeply rising ground . . . recent heavy chafings as from the sliding pressure of footwear were noted at the bottom of the trees by which the clothing lay but no other major disturbances as from a struggle involved on the adjacent ground.'

(c)   Detective Inspector Dean said:
'Assuming that a man and a woman had used the mackintosh as a bed and the coat as a pillow their feet would have been against the tree (looking at photograph 5), that is if they were lying across the raincoat. If they had been lying down the slope their heads would have been nearer the tree.'

(d)   George William Brown said in cross-examination:
'Photos 5 and 6 were taken on 11 August. The chafing marks were fresh.'

(e)   Detective Inspector Dean said:
'On August 10 1948 . . . I went to Box Copse . . . I there saw the body of a dead woman . . . Standing by the clothing it was possible to see the body where it lay, part of it was obscured but it was possible to see that it was a body . . . It was obvious by just glancing at the legs that it was the body of a youngish woman.'

(f)   Frederick George Chamberlain's account of a conversation with Thomas Stillwell:
'I've just found a body in the park. I said, "Do you mean somebody dead?" and he said, "Yes, a woman." I asked him if it was an old woman and he said, "No, I should say she would about 25 or 27." He may have said 27 or 28, I'm not exactly certain. He said that he'd reported it to the police.'

(g) John Albert Mobey's account of a conversation with Thomas Stillwell: 'I know the accused Stillwell. I remember on the day of the inquest seeing him on Arundel Bridge. There was some conversation between us, it was about the murder. He said he goes to the pictures on a Saturday. I could not say why he said that to me . . . Later on I saw him in Littlehampton . . . about a week later . . . There was more conversation about the murder, he said he couldn't say where he was. He didn't say in relation to anything or on what occasion. We were talking about the murder when he made that observation.'

In my opinion the circumstantial evidence pointing to the conclusion that Stillwell raped Miss Woodhouse in Box Copse is beyond reasonable doubt and therefore proposition 2(2) is established. The following are my reasons namely:

(1) There is uncontradicted evidence that Miss Woodhouse was a woman of good character and that she was raped and strangled.

(2) There is evidence that Stillwell entered Box Copse about the time she did; that Stillwell followed here there e.g., 'When I climbed the slope at the end of Box Copse I could see her.'
That Stillwell had been following her for some time e.g., 'the girl I had been following'.
That Stillwell was sexually excited by her.
That Stillwell said he was 'hot-blooded'.
That after speaking to her he went away and masturbated.
That this was no impediment to a second immediate erection as in the case of his several affairs with the other girl Mary, e.g., 'and then became erect again'.
That Stillwell had frequently exposed his person indecently to others in Arundel Park.
That Stillwell wondered where Clements and Challen were; walked up the bank to see where they were; must have known from their direction that they were walking away from Box Copse.

(3) There is no evidence of any other man in or near Box Copse at the relevant time although there is abundant evidence to account for the movements of all other persons in the vicinity at the time.

(4)   There is evidence that Stillwell on seeing the girl's body was able to fix the girl's age (23, 27 or 28 per Chamberlain's evidence) with greater accuracy than Detective Inspector Dean (who said she was a 'youngish woman') although her face was decomposed.

(5)   Stillwell's conversation with Mobey looks like an attempt to prepare an alibi.

(6)   Stillwell went immediately after 4 p.m. to the neighbouring town of Littlehampton and there bought a new shirt. The fact that just that particular afternoon Stillwell decided to buy a new shirt, and that he did not buy it in the town of Arundel, that he journeyed to Littlehampton for the new shirt and that the old shirt was not accounted for, taken in conjunction with the other facts of the case seem to be more than coincidental.

(7)   This is my new point in the case. There is evidence that the assailant carried out the rape on his left side and from her right side.

In RV Clewew (1830) 4. C&P p. 221 the following facts were held to be relevant as showing A's identity; that B's wounds must have been inflicted by a left-handed man and that A was left-handed.

In the present case there is evidence that the assailant carried out the rape on his left side and from her right side.

That the assailant carried out the rape on his left side is manifest from the medical evidence and from the photographic evidence indicating the injuries to the deceased, particularly the bruises on her legs. Those bruises are mainly on the inside of her left leg indicating that it was the left leg that was pushed apart from its inner side. Other bruises of a different kind seem to suggest that the assailant lay across the deceased's right leg.

The habit of most men, I am informed, is to have sexual intercourse from their right side and not from their left side. That is because with most men the testicles hang towards the left leg. Thus all tailors know that most men 'dress left'. The makers of DAKS trousers, I am informed, mass produce trousers for men who 'dress left'. The ratio of men whose testicles hang right and who prefer to have intercourse on the left is, I am informed, very small.

As I have said the evidence in this case indicates that the assailant committed the rape from his left side. What conclusions may be safely drawn from that fact? Either of two conclusions are, in my opinion, irresistible. They are that the assailant was either:

(a) a man who 'dresses right' and therefore approaches intercourse from the left; or

(b) a man who at the time of the murder was under a physical handicap making it impossible or difficult or painful to carry out rape on his right side, and who perforce was compelled when committing rape, to rape on his unnatural left side.

Stillwell on 17 October 1948 said:

'On 12 April 1948 I fractured my leg playing football; it was the left leg and it was fractured at the ankle. My foot is still a bit weak.'

Narborough said:

'The recent heavy chafing as from the sliding pressure of footwear were noted at the bottom of the trunks of several box trees by which the clothing lay, but no other major disturbances as from a struggle involved in the ground adjacent.'

Detective Inspector Dean said:

'I noticed on the trees at the foot of the clothing recent heavy chafing marks some 18 inches from the ground.'

The evidence in my view points to the following conclusions:

That she was raped where her clothing lay by a man whose footwear chafed the adjacent trees.

That the assailant raped her from the right, i.e. from her left, that after the rape she ran, was overtaken and strangled where her body was found.

But evidence relevant to this aspect of the case which is not before me include:

evidence or marks of any man's footwear;

evidence as to whether the chafings are by that footwear;

evidence as to which side of the clothing the trees were.

As it stands the evidence points to Stillwell as her assailant for the reasons already given that at the relevant period:

(1) he was sexually excited by her and followed her into Box Copse;

(2) the weakness in his left leg;

(3) that her assailant attacked her from the left;

(4) that Stillwell seems to have tried to prepare an alibi;

(5) that Stillwell stated her approximate age with greater precision than an experienced police officer.

3.   **Matters left unexplained.**

Although the evidence available at present points strongly to the guilt of Stillwell there are several matters left unexplained in this strange case. There is no evidence of Stillwell's:

> clothing or footwear;
>
> scratches or other injury to his person;
>
> 'poisoned finger' its cause, duration or nature;
>
> fingerprints on any article;
>
> pubic hairs;
>
> seminal fluids on his or her garments;
>
> old shirt he wore on 31 July 1948 before he bought a new one the same afternoon;
>
> remark to the witness Mobey that he goes to the pictures on Saturday.

Further there is no explanation as to the absence of the Lembar bottle. Further evidence on these matters now unexplained might, perhaps, establish beyond reasonable doubt the innocence of Thomas Stillwell.

In the absence of such evidence the statements at present before me point strongly towards the guilt of Thomas Stillwell and for the reasons I have given I am of the opinion that before any application is made for leave to prefer a Bill of Indictment the DPP should, with respect, be invited to consider the aspects of the case which I have indicated.

In this opinion some of the evidence has been necessarily repeated more than once but under different headings in order to make clearer my view of its relevance to the particular aspect of the case being examined.

HECTOR HUGHES
21 November 1950
1, Garden Court

At 5,000 words it is a repetitive (as Hughes acknowledged) and some-times poorly structured counsel's opinion. The new evidence or information that was a key requirement of filing for a Bill of Indictment was also fairly flimsy. The contention that if Joan Woodhouse was raped from the right side and Stillwell had a leg injury that would make him more likely to perform a rape from that side proves little.

However, if the point was to put in front of Justice Humphreys the content of Stillwell's confessions to sexual deviancy and the real reasons why he was in the park on the day of the murder more fully, then it would have served its purpose.

Reading between the lines, Hughes knew that the real card to be played was the issue of the loss of potential evidence by police that degraded the case: the boots, the Lembar bottle, the shirt, etc. Yet, if he made police incompetence the thrust of his opinion or even stated it explicitly, then the likelihood is that Justice Humphreys – a died-in-the-wool upholder of the Establishment – would knock it back with little consideration. He therefore presented all this at the end of his opinion under 'Matters left unexplained'.

Travers Humphreys, the man who would make the final decision as to whether justice for Joan would be allowed to be pursued, was by now eighty-three years old. He had a long and illustrious career behind him and was now sitting as the senior judge in the Court of Appeal. His son was Christmas Humphreys, QC, a leading prosecuting lawyer. Away from his legal career Christmas was an enthusiastic Buddhist and founded what became the London Buddhist Society and authored a number of works on the subject. He became senior prosecuting counsel for the Crown in 1950 and he would soon come to public prominence. He led for the Crown in the Craig and Bentley case in 1952, prosecuted Ruth Ellis a few years later and secured the conviction of Timothy Evans for a murder he may not have committed. The Craig and Bentley case was the subject of the film *Let Him Have It*. Bentley, who would today be classified as having special needs, was hanged because he was over eighteen, while his accomplice in a burglary, sixteen-year-old Christopher Craig, escaped the noose even though it was he, alone, that shot a policeman during the course of the robbery. Ruth Ellis was the last British woman to be executed and today her shooting of her gallivanting lover would have probably got her a suspended sentence. In the cases of Bentley and Ellis, their executions led to a groundswell of opinion against capital punishment.

On this occasion, though, Judge Travers Humphreys was taking no risks of a potential miscarriage of justice. In a letter received by Mr Dickinson in

Hull on Saturday 2 December 1950 he was informed that Justice Humphreys had refused leave to prefer a bill of indictment against a named person. All legal channels had now been exhausted. In 1950 there was no European Court to appeal to. The end of the road had been reached. There was nowhere left to go.

22
AFTERMATH

The family were, naturally, distraught. There were no twenty-four-hour rolling-news channels to breathe life into the case, and the popular newspapers were not about to adopt the Woodhouse's fight as a *cause célèbre*. In 1950 the belief that the British judicial system was the best in the world still held firm, and the general public still strongly felt that the police force was fundamentally decent, if occasionally inept. Most of all, the usual run of things was for newspapers to campaign for people they believed had been wrongly convicted of crimes not to lobby to have somebody convicted and hanged.

There was, however, great pity for the family, but there was a school of thought in the media, and perhaps among the public, that they had been given a good crack of the whip in pursuing the suspect and had not been able to produce enough evidence. If the police maintained that they could not charge the man, then they must be right. If he were guilty what possible reason could they have not to prosecute? The public opinion over their police force was still a quarter of a century away from being recalibrated following the widespread Scotland Yard corruption and 'canteen-culture' revelations of the 1960s onwards. And names such as Stephen Lawrence, Harry Stanley and Ian Tomlinson and the connotations these have with regard to public trust in the police and their ability to look inwards were even further in the future

In desperation the family and close friends began sending out final pleading letters, finding it excruciating to accept that the cause was now finally lost. Lena Bamber wrote to George Oliver, the former long-serving MP for Ilkeston, and who was now a King's Counsel, and would have been dismayed to receive the following reply on 5 December 1950, which began:

Dear Miss Barber [sic],
I have delayed replying to the letter which you were good enough to send
respecting the case of Miss Joan Greenwood [sic] . . .

Lena's name was *Bamber*, and Joan Greenwood was a glamorous British
actress who had recently starred in the film *Whisky Galore!* The fact that
the parliamentarian had got his constituent's name wrong and mixed up
the subject of the letter with a sex symbol indicated where his mind may
have been at the time. In his defence he was another member of the Establishment who was in his ninth decade when the correspondence took
place.

On the 14 January 1951 the family collaborated on their final letter to
the director of public prosecutions:

Dear Sir
Since we received our final blow sickness has prevented our writing to you.

We only now realise just how futile our fight for right and justice has been
from the beginning. Why do we pretend to have law in our country whereby
wrongs may be righted, and because absolute power is there, authority can
render useless individual efforts to obtain justice and, adding insult to injury,
allude to our fight as 'persecution'.

We do not accept the statement of 'inadequate evidence'. We took steps
to be assured that there was. Four highly experienced legal minds on
Criminal Law are agreed on this, even after taking into account the vital clues
allowed to be lost. The least we could have expected was that what did
remain should have been used to the full in a crime so outrageous and cruel.

Is the Opinion of KC also considered of no account? After all that is
known this case could never be truly unsolved and placed against those on
files [sic]. If it were it would be monstrous.

With revenge we are not concerned but a wretched sex pervert outraged
the pure body of a saintly girl and because she fought for the things in which
she believed, for his foul lust he cut off her precious young life. Surely it was
little enough to expect that at least the menace was removed from society
and given time to atone – if he understands the meaning of the word – for
his evil deed.

After reading the Opinion of KC one of Joan's friends remarked: 'Shame, repulsion and fury were reactions. To think that such a beast is "man" and, too, that he is still at large when out of his own mouth he is condemned is galling indeed.' And that is the reaction of all concerned.

Trust the British public to raise their voice against injustice – 'You have had a ghastly deal . . . I have never known a grosser injustice since the Dreyfus case . . .' – this evidently bears comparison with the treatment we have received though we never knew the case.

We are, Sir,

Yours faithfully,

J.T Woodhouse

Annie Blades and Ida Sheriff

The Dreyfus affair – albeit unfamiliar to John Woodhouse – referred to by one of the family's sympathisers did bear some similarity to Joan's case with regard to the fight the Woodhouse family found themselves in with the Establishment.

Captain Alfred Dreyfus was a young French soldier of German and Jewish descent who was imprisoned on Devil's Island for allegedly leaking French military secrets to the German Embassy in Paris in 1894. Dreyfus' family were convinced of his innocence and began to campaign for a retrial. They were strongly resisted, even when it emerged that a French Army major was the real culprit. Instead of admitting to a mistake, senior French Army officials suppressed the information and even went on to accuse Dreyfus of more offences. If John Woodhouse had been *au fait* with this famous case he would undoubtedly have seen parallels between the French Army and Scotland Yard. In 1906, twelve years after his conviction, Dreyfus was finally exonerated of everything, and he lived out a blameless life, with the case becoming one of the first and most famous (or notorious) miscarriages of justice of all time.

Soon after the final rebuttal the case of Joan Woodhouse's murder receded from the public mind except for those who knew and loved the troubled young lady. There were a few triggers that revived it over the following years, but, bearing in mind the enormous publicity the case had generated, it all but disappeared. This may have been down to the unusual circumstances, namely that it would be difficult to refer to the case in much detail without mentioning the chief suspect, who was never charged with the murder. The media may have been exercising some responsibility towards Thomas Stillwell.

In February 1951 the *Sunday Chronicle* reported that a woman had come forward to a London solicitor implicating as Joan's killer a man that visited Worthing regularly to play golf but had not been seen there since the murder. It was a flimsy premise for a front-page story and was not followed up, presumably because it was a dead end.

Sam Jackett, a celebrated crime reporter, who would later write a book called *Heroes of Scotland Yard*, examined the case in the *Derby Evening Telegraph* of 9 January 1953. For the first time he referred to a series of anonymous letters apparently received by Scotland Yard:

> In the meantime the mystery had become even more puzzling, because of a series of anonymous letters which reached Scotland Yard and which had obviously been written by someone who had known the dead girl quite well. But despite appeals from the officers in charge of the case the writer steadfastly refused to divulge his identity. All efforts to trace him were without avail, and to this day he remains as unknown as his association (if any) with the crime.
>
> The murderer of this devout and happy girl remains unknown. Could the writer of the anonymous letters help? It is never too late.

This should have been an explosive assertion. Jackett was presenting a new suspect, albeit anonymous, and referring to evidence that had not been in the public domain – if it did exist. Also where and to whom did these Scotland Yard officers appeal? There is no record of any such appeal in the national media. Even more strangely, neither Spooner nor Narborough refer to these letters in their literary accounts of the case. There are no letters from the family among their otherwise comprehensive files, although the article itself is there. They either disregarded it or were weary of such red herrings by this time.

The *Sunday Pictorial* ran a story on 18 March 1956, which went as far to say that the case was being reopened on the strength of a woman overhearing a conversation. The *Pictorial*'s crime reporter claimed that detectives were flying to the Continent to interview a man who formerly lived in southern England. Again, no follow-up or conclusion was ever presented.

On 7 and 9 April 1956 *The Times* reported that a man had been interviewed in Rhodesia in connection with the murder of Joan Woodhouse. Whether this was part of the same lead as that in the *Sunday Pictorial* is not clear. A man, they wrote, had confessed, and Scotland Yard had established that he had lived in the Arundel area at the time of the murder. When this author appealed for information on the murder in the columns of the Littlehampton, Arundel and Worthing press in 2010 one anonymous correspondent expressed anger that Thomas Stillwell was able to start a new life in South Africa on the money received from selling his story and that he was soon 'chucked out of there'. The letter writer may well have had it wrong because, as far as this author knows, Thomas Stillwell lived out his entire life in Arundel.

In 1966 a magazine splashed a story claiming that a journalist had 'solved' the Joan Woodhouse murder case. The journalist was Iain Adamson, and he was publicising his new book on Inspector Spooner *The Great Detective*. The policeman had died in September 1963.

Here it was claimed for the first time that Spooner believed that Joan committed suicide and was not murdered. He insisted that nobody at the Yard believed that Joan's murderer even existed. He must then have been ignoring Fred Narborough's earlier book and obviously had no knowledge of what Spooner had said in private to the Woodhouse family and Lena Bamber.

In the book Spooner suggests that Professor Keith Simpson was fallible and that Joan's body was so decomposed that he could have been mistaken about her injuries. The family would argue that this assertion only makes the case against Stillwell more powerful. George Chamberlain, the publican of the Black Rabbit, had testified that Stillwell had said to him he had found the body and that it was a girl of twenty-six or twewnty-seven. If she was as decomposed as Spooner now suggested how could he have known that?

Perhaps more significant for the Woodhouse family was something else that the book revealed: in a respectful way it discloses that Spooner was a seriously heavy drinker throughout his later police career and that his alcoholism contributed to his premature death. Could his illness have clouded his judgement and his ability to carry out his job at this point in his career?

Dr Simpson was not happy about Spooner's assertion. Scotland Yard would always aver to the pathologist's skills and experience, and here was a policeman he had worked with many times saying that his conclusions on this case were possibly shaky. Simpson would simply point out that there was another pathologist on the case who agreed with him and point to the injuries to the neck that were consistent with strangling. An independent observer would ask why Spooner should expound the suicide theory in later life yet never suggested this as even a possibility when he was drafted into the revisit the case in 1950.

However, the suicide theory should not be completely discounted. Joan had suffered from depression in the months before the August bank holiday; the ending of the relationship with Ted Roberts had affected her deeply. She had sought counsel with her priest, and she had gone to her aunts in Bridlington for solace. She had even confessed to contemplating suicide (although she was later horrified by this) and there is a brief reference in one letter to an incident when Joan's aunts thought she may have made an attempt with pills. It was the first thing that Ida Sheriff thought when she heard of Joan's demise. In a letter to the Superintendent of Police, Arundel, dated 21 August 1948, she writes:

> I expect you will think it is fantastic that I should ask you if there is any possibility that Joan might have taken her own life? The depression we saw in her because of the religious upheaval she was passing through brought about by Ted Roberts being adamant that she should practice [sic] or at least adhere to his beliefs (this is my version, not Joan's) we feel because of her great love for him we expect that might be the answer rather than this. Her letter of 11-1-48 shows clearly what she was passing through.

Joan's behaviour on the day of her death could be interpreted as that of someone who had decided to take their own life. Friends and relatives of suicide victims have frequently noted that their loved ones showed a degree of buoyancy and serenity immediately before their deaths. This is attributed to the fact that a decision has been made and the terrible burden of depression has been lifted.

Joan headed off for a place that reminded her of happier times and sought a secluded spot to take her life. She even took off and folded her clothes and made a makeshift bed. Perhaps she had hoped that animals would have devoured her corpse before some unfortunate person found her.

This is all fine, but how are the injuries and evidence of a struggle explained? To believe that someone came upon Joan after she had committed suicide and interfered with her body is a belief too far. Why would that person need to struggle with a corpse or apply severe pressure to her neck and damage her voice-box? It does not stand up.

Also, if Joan was really heading down to Arundel that sunny day to end her life would she have really purchased a newspaper and two women's magazines to read on the way, even if she was calm about what she was going to do?

Finally, although there were some traces of aspirin in her body it was a small dose. The suicide theory, while worthy of consideration, simply does not have real legs. Joan was depressed. She was fragile. She may have been mentally disorientated on the weekend of her death, but that does not mean she committed suicide or had that in mind.

This brings us back to the premise that Joan was murdered and inevitably to Thomas Stillwell. What are the odds of a man with a habit of molesting women and exposing himself meeting up with the murder victim on one day *and* being the person who discovered her dead body some days later?

There are no other known suspects; no other unidentified men seen in the vicinity. Stillwell was himself the only witness to mention a man with field glasses being in the park on the day of the murder. Was this an attempt by him to throw in an imaginary voyeur-suspect into the pot? Not taking into account all the other circumstantial evidence, the sheer coincidence of Stillwell being someone whose sexual compulsions were demonstrably running high at the time of the killing and meeting Joan on the day of her murder and then finding her body is almost beyond credible.

23
PARALLELS

It is dangerous to condemn a person on the powerful persuasiveness of coincidence alone. Nearly half a century after Thomas Stillwell was accused of Joan Woodhouse's murder a case that has some striking similarities serves to make us all cautious in situations such as this. Or, at least, it should.

On a hot summer's day in 1992 Rachel Nickell was stabbed forty-nine times and killed on Wimbledon Common in London while her two-year-old son looked on. It was a horrific murder in broad daylight at a well-known beauty spot, and the media and public alike were alarmed and frightened and immense pressure was piled upon the police to make an early arrest.

They quickly responded by identifying Colin Stagg as their suspect. He was an oddball, a loner who lived across the A3 main road from the common on a Roehampton council estate and was known to sunbathe naked and sometimes masturbate near where Rachel was attacked. He, too, admitted to having been at the scene on the day of the murder.

Like Stillwell, here was a man who was 'perverted', who admitted to being near the scene and at the time of the murder. This level of coincidence was compelling to the police, the media and the public.

However, there was no forensic or significant circumstantial evidence, and Stagg vehemently denied the charge. Scotland Yard resorted to setting a honeytrap for him. There are parallels here with Inspector Narborough's sending the family and friends of Joan Woodhouse out on to the streets of Arundel. A policewoman was tasked with befriending him, initially by letter – Stagg had become a public-hate figure by now – and coaxing him into confessing to Rachel's murder. Despite the policewoman – who Stagg believed was a lady called Lizzie Jones – pretending to 'get off' sexually on violence, he never admitted to anything.

Nevertheless, the police pursued him further and charged him with murder in the summer of 1993, and his case reached the Old Bailey in September of the following year.

Mr Justice Ognall had not allowed himself to be caught up in the hysteria surrounding the case and the national and almost complete demonization of Stagg. He cast a cold, legal eye over the actual prosecution case. He excluded the evidence gathered during the entrapment process, saying the police had shown excessive zeal and that the attempt to incriminate a suspect was deceptive conduct of the grossest kind. Colin Stagg was acquitted and left the court to face an uncertain future.

The police announced that they were not seeking anyone else in connection with the murder, which was as good as passing the sentence the court could not. It is, as mentioned earlier, a traditional way for the police to say the court is wrong – we are right; we have the right man.

Stagg was resolute and refused to leave his flat despite the risks of retribution and misplaced vigilantism. He merely wanted to walk his dog on Wimbledon Common once more. But he faced the worst possible nightmare. The country believed him to be guilty. In the collective mind he looked and acted guilty, and there was barely a dissenting voice to be heard. Most believed that it was only a matter of time before a self-styled avenger or a gang dispensed people's justice on Stagg.

This author had personal experience of the general hysteria. My daughter attended a local senior girls' school at the time, and there was a strong rumour that Colin Stagg had been seen walking his dog in the local park. The headmistress called an assembly and advised her pupils not to walk across the park to and from school. Panicky parents began to ferry their children around. It transpired that Stagg had never been in the vicinity. Colin Stagg was the monster in our midst, and his liberty was deemed intolerable.

It took nearly another ten years for Colin Stagg to be proved entirely innocent. DNA profiling had revealed that a man named Robert Napper, already incarcerated in Broadmoor Hospital for two murders, was the killer of Rachel Nickell. Colin Stagg received an apology from the police and later a financial award. No amount of money could be adequate compensation, though, for nearly twenty years of persecution, misery and fear.

Fortunately for Stagg, after some years, the media moved on and the murder of TV presenter Jill Dando in 1999 gave focus to a new hate figure,

Barry George, the man suspected (by the police at least) and later convicted of shooting her. George was another oddball who had the misfortune to live close to the scene of the murder.

As with Stagg there was tremendous pressure on the police to find the killer, exacerbated by the fact that Dando was a presenter of BBC's crime appeal programme *Crimewatch*. George was popularly believed to be guilty mainly because he had an obsession with Freddie Mercury, the Queen singer, and had a copy of the *Radio Times* in his flat that had Jill Dando on the cover. It was barely mentioned that he hoarded scores of other copies of the *Radio Times*, too.

Barry George was also later pardoned after an appeal court ruled him to be innocent. To date he has not been awarded compensation for his wrongful imprisonment, although he has won damages from some newspaper organisations.

Stillwell's perceived culpability was even more compelling than that of Stagg. Stillwell admitted to seeing and following the victim on the day of the murder and later found her body. He was not merely a sexual deviant who was in the right place at the right time. The crucial difference in the two cases was that with Stillwell the police did not want to convict, it seems, whereas with Stagg they did.

With Stillwell, too, there was another element not present with Stagg: putting the sheer level of coincidence to one side, there is also the volume of circumstantial evidence and its absence to consider. What happened to Stillwell's shirt? What made him decide to buy a new one on the day of the murder and why did he make that the last thing he did that afternoon and not the first? What were the clothes being washed by Stillwell's aunt, and was it ever really investigated as to whether it was usual for her to take in washing for her relative? Why did Stillwell lie about why he was at Box Copse when he discovered the body? Why did he say to police that Joan's death must have been his fault? How was he able to estimate almost exactly the age of the body he found when pathologists agreed that Joan's features were badly damaged through decomposition? What were the exact circumstances of the injury to his hand? Were his strange conversations with another villager a clumsy attempt at constructing an alibi? Stillwell admitted that, on finding the body, he searched the dead woman's pockets. Is this the normal behaviour on finding a dead body? How many other examples of a witness stumbling on a corpse doing this are there? Surely, one would recoil in horror and alert the police as quickly aspossible.

Is there not then another possibility? That if Stillwell was composed enough to search the dead woman's clothing, could he have been the one who folded it up neatly and not Joan? (In 2015 Nicole Ashby expressed scepticism over whether the Paisley dress was ever really neatly folded, saying, 'When I went to Scotland Yard to identify the clothes, that dress had been dropped on the ground, and if the pathologist said it was neatly put on the ground, heaven knows what his house looked like!')

Why then, when there was far more reason for the police to believe that Stillwell was guilty than there was years later in the case of Stagg, did they not pursue him in the same way they did his 1990s equivalent? It cannot have been in the apparent weaknesses in the case against him but must have been rooted in the investigation itself. What other possible reason could there have been? There was no threat to national security. No notable people to protect. No money changing hands. The family suspected at the time – as did Thomas Jacks, Hector Hughes and a handful of others – that the only possible conclusion was that the police had something to hide.

It is this author's conclusion, too, that Scotland Yard botched the early stages of the investigation – would or could not face up to this fact – and dug themselves in deeper and deeper. They had not banked on the family's tenacity and that the road would lead to a private prosecution, and that eventuality prompted the Establishment to swing into action and squash it and the family in the process.

Inspector Narborough's autobiography *Murder On My Mind* is revelatory. The murder of Joan Woodhouse dominates the entire book. The cover blurb itself says 'overshadowing all these is his preoccupation with the Arundel case'. Joan's picture is the inside-cover plate, and the book opens and closes with the case.

In my view it drips with apology rather than defensiveness. There is a passage, though, seemingly unrelated to the investigation that may also be significant. Fred Narborough reveals that during the war, as a senior police detective, he was put on war work:

So I found myself with Mr Hartley Shawcross, who had been a busy King's Counsel on the northern circuit, in a church hall off Finchley Road, NW 11.

Our job was to screen the many aliens who had flocked to the Golders Green area. The task took all of six months.

He goes on to describe how the pair of them sat together, day in day out, interrogating 'alien' suspects and concludes:

Every time I reach for a cigarette nowadays I recall Dunkirk and the dangerous months of 1940. The solid silver case I have is inscribed 'To FN from HWS to commemorate a very pleasant association on T12'.

What Sir Hartley did not tell me was that he had written to Sir Norman Kendal praising in lavish phrase the work of his temporary secretary (me) in the church hall.

Narborough could not be clearer that a mutual appreciation society had been formed between the policeman and the barrister. Ten years later Hartley Shawcross was the attorney general, the chief legal adviser to the Crown, and the man who could and did direct the legal Establishment's policy on the Joan Woodhouse case. How would he have reacted when he received the letter from Joan's aunts on the 23 September 1950 referring to 'the blind, stupid blundering of Scotland Yard'? This was his friend they were maligning, a good copper, FN, to whom he had gifted a silver cigarette case and with whom he had bonded over six months doing their bit together for the war effort.

His impulse may have been to rail back at the family's grievances, and it could be argued that he did just that. It is certainly unimaginable that his friendship with Narborough, who stood to be totally discredited if the Woodhouse case went to the Old Bailey, did not colour his thinking when considering how to proceed over the thorny issue of Thomas Stillwell and the murder of Joan Woodhouse.

Another case that bears mention and shows parallels is that of Vera Page. Vera was a ten-year-old girl from Notting Hill, London, who was found raped and strangled a mile from her home in 1921. Clues were sparse, but an ammonia-stained finger bandage was found near the body. Percy Orlando Rush emerged as a prime suspect. He was a forty-year-old man who had been seen lurking in the area and had recently had a bandage applied to his finger and worked with ammonia. It also emerged that Rush's clothing was semen-stained and that he had previous offences for indecent exposure to young girls. Yet, in the absence of anybody seeing him with young Vera or in the immediate vicinity at the right time the police decided not to lay charges – and in this case there was no backdrop of a possible flawed investigation.

Another, more recent, parallel is that of the racist killing of Stephen Lawrence in Plumstead, London, in April 1993. Lawrence was a nineteen-year-old black teenager who was randomly attacked, stabbed and killed by a white gang at a bus stop. As with the Stillwell case there was strong local knowledge or opinion as to who was responsible for the murder, and the police eventually charged two suspects, but the CPS dropped the case in July 1993 citing insufficient evidence.

They had not bargained for the campaign waged by Stephen's parents, Doreen and Neville Lawrence, who, as with the Woodhouse family nearly fifty years earlier, became exasperated with the police and launched the first private prosecution for murder since John Woodhouse's in 1950.

This time the case did get to trial, and the charges against the two original suspects were dropped through lack of evidence, and the three remaining suspects (identified by the private prosecution) were acquitted when the judge ruled that identification evidence given by a witness was inadmissible. The family had to face the extra pain of witnessing a TV programme that had covertly filmed the suspects laughing about the killing and seemingly re-enacting the stabbing. Later the *Daily Mail* named all five and accused them of murder, inviting them to sue them for libel if they were innocent. The suspects did not react.

The Lawrence family demanded an inquiry into the police handling of the case. This time the complaint was not principally incompetence followed by a cover-up, as in the Arundel inquiry, but racism on the part of the police. Although no officers faced any real punishment the Macpherson Report that followed found that the police were institutionally racist as well as incompetent. They were accused of not following up obvious leads, and a number of recommendations were made to address the deficiencies.

In his award-winning book on the whole affair, *The Case Of Stephen Lawrence*, Brian Cathcart makes the following observations about private prosecutions for murder:

Doreen and Neville had been talking for nine months about a private prosecution, but in reality this was a very long shot. Private prosecutions were rare, and for good reasons: the legal authorities frowned on them *and even obstructed them* [author's italics], while the costs to the plaintiff could be ruinous. Private prosecutions for murder were virtually unknown; there had been just three in 130 years.

In 1950, when the Woodhouse private prosecution was mounted, the notion that the legal process was anything but fair and historically rooted in British principles of justice for all was unthinkable. Mr Bass's insipid performance as a prosecutor, knowing what we do now, does not surprise. By the end of the century it was no longer a given that the legal Establishment was truly independent and *at all times* honourable.

Stephen Lawrence's family did finally win some justice for their son. In 2012 two of the gang had their acquittals quashed and were sentenced to fifteen and fourteen years' imprisonment. New forensic evidence and changes in double-jeopardy laws were cited as the catalyst for the new convictions, but political will may have played its part. Speculation remains that the other gang members will, sooner or later, face justice.

A 2014 report on the affair by Mark Ellison, QC, revealed that the police had placed a covert spy in the Lawrence family camp while they were fighting for justice. It also disclosed that files of evidence were destroyed and confirmed that ties existed between the alleged gangster father of one of the suspects and police officers. The story goes on.

All these developments and revelations show how Scotland Yard closed ranks and demonstrably considered the Lawrence family, and not the perpetrators of the crime, to be the enemy. They stopped at almost nothing to prevent their shortcomings, prejudices and even corruption being probed and exposed.

Admittedly there are almost fifty years separating the two cases, but a culture at Scotland Yard such as the one that the Lawrence case highlighted did not spring up overnight. It was entrenched over the years, and the 'Porn Squad' convictions of the 1970s are proof of this.

The author spoke to a former criminal, now in his nineties, who was active in the late 1940s through to the early 1960s. He served several prison sentences and had links to some leading south-London criminals who found notoriety in the 1960s and 1970s. He has led a law-abiding life for the last fifty years but was able to talk about the culture at Scotland Yard around the time of Joan's murder.

We knew the leading detectives as well as they knew us. They often came from the same streets as us. We'd been through the war together. There was a mutual respect. There were two coppers who were in the Flying Squad we dealt with a lot. One of them became a household name. We used to drive up to the Albion pub by Ludgate Circus and hand over cash. They knew we were on various jobs, and we paid them off. The same coppers would take us to a lock-up at the old Scotland Yard building and let us buy goods they had seized from people like us.

I was never fitted up. But I knew people that were. You were likely to get fitted up if you stepped outside the arrangements. Or if you crossed the line and mugged them off in some way. They didn't like to be made to look stupid. Detectives lied on oath regularly, nearly as much we did.

Looking back on it, we didn't even consider them corrupt. They were doing a job, as we were. We were all trying to make a pound note. Most of them were decent men. I was always surprised when all the Scotland Yard bent-coppers stuff started coming out in the 1960s and 70s, and the *News Of The World* was up in arms and so was the public. The papers knew – the police had been giving them stories for years – and I was shocked the public were shocked.

I remember the Joan Woodhouse case but didn't pay much attention. Never had much interest in sex crimes. Would the police let a suspected murderer go free if it meant his pursuit would show a senior detective in an unflattering light? I can't speak for other forces, but Scotland Yard in the 1950s? Of course. Without a doubt. They wouldn't allow one of theirs to be hung out to dry. Never.

Some sixty-seven years later it is unthinkable that Joan's family and friends will ever see justice. Almost everybody connected to the case is now dead. The conclusion that Thomas Stillwell got away with murder is hard to refute. He possibly escaped Albert Pierrepoint and his noose not because of any particular ingenuity on his part or a wavering jury, but because of two things: first, the incompetence of the initial police inquiry and the refusal to acknowledge this and make amends; and, second, the Establishment's terror of a private prosecution for murder ever succeeding and all that would have meant for the system.

24
A LIKELY SCENARIO

Having read as much as I can lay my hands on the Arundel murder, examining police files, interviewing surviving friends of Joan and relatives of people involved in the case and turning over everything in my mind time and time again, my belief is that what happened to Joan on the hot, stifling day in 1948 went along the following lines.

Joan had been depressed by the collapse of her relationship with Ted Roberts and felt pressurised by the demands of her religious commitment. Nevertheless, she had decided to return home to Barnsley to her father's house or to her aunts in Bridlington on the bank-holiday Saturday of August 1948.

She set off from Blackheath in the morning but faced unprecedented crowds pouring into London for the opening of the Olympic Games. She decided against battling them on the rail network in the intense, unbearable heat and decided to travel down to Worthing or Arundel and spend some of the day there before travelling north in the later afternoon or early evening. By then the crush would have subsided, and she would have a stress-free, cooler journey home.

Joan was familiar with and fond of both Worthing and Arundel – her beloved aunts having lived in the former and all having enjoyed picnics at the latter. She had been disappointed that petrol rationing had scuppered a planned visit to Arundel earlier in the year with her aunts. She thought it would be nice to be able to see them in Bridlington and announce, 'You'll never guess where I've been . . . Arundel!'

She purchased a newspaper and a couple of magazines for the various train journeys. On arrival at Arundel she bought a cooling drink and set off in the direction of Swanbourne Lake in the grounds of Arundel Castle. She knew she was going to head for Box Copse because she, Ida and Annie had picnicked many times on the hill leading up to it. She had a purpose for going there. Number 6 in her Rule of Life read as follows:

Make one-quarter-of-an-hour meditations each week and make an annual retreat.

She would take the opportunity to do this at Box Copse. In the park she was waylaid by a man. He tried to engage her in conversation, but there was something unsettling about him, and she did not respond. He abused her, told her, 'Well, bugger you, then.' Not wishing to encourage or incite him any way she walked on without looking over her shoulder.

She didn't really give it a thought as she climbed the hill to Box Copse. The man who had watched her ascend the steep slope was distracted when he spoke to two men from the village he knew. But he was sexually excited and felt that the girl might be one of those who feign lack of interest but really wanted something. Why climb up to such a secluded spot alone? When the coast was clear he followed and sought out the girl's position. He was brought to a state of high arousal when he saw that she had taken off her outer clothes and was lying in her underwear on her back with her coat as a pillow.

Joan was meditating, in touch with her God, but to Thomas Stillwell, oversexed and deluded about his own physical magnetism, she was prepared for a sexual encounter. Women found him irresistible, he believed, but this situation was most unusual. His penis was out and he was masturbating as he stood over her and spoke. Joan opened her eyes and screamed at him and tried to scramble away.

The local man Stillwell pursued and pulled her quickly to the ground urgently prodding at her vagina with his penis and fingers. Joan was resisting and was shouting and screaming. This looked bad. This looked like rape. He had never gone this far before. He stuffed his fingers into her mouth and she bit hard. He had ejaculated now and panicked. Sexually sated, the enormity of the situation enveloped him. His other hand was already around the girl's throat, and she was continuing to writhe and struggle. He could not let her go. There were people on the path at the bottom of the hill. He'd be for it. Nobody would believe him if he said he had been led on. He intensified his grip. It seemed to take an age for her to stop biting and kicking. When she did, she was dead.

He stood up and surveyed the situation. He thought about covering the body but decided against it. He looked in her handbag and her pockets and took out a return railway ticket to London. She was a visitor. He tidied her clothes and hair. Tried to make it look less like a struggle. He emerged from Box Copse, checking first to see if anyone was going to see him. Then he ran down the hill and got on to the path where he walked normally. He noticed his shirt was torn in the struggle and there were specks of blood on it. Buttoning his jacket he decided to get to Hepworths in Littlehampton and buy a new one. On leaving the shop he put the new shirt on and disposed of the stained one. He went to the pictures and played darts at the Black Rabbit, careful to demonstrate that he had carried on as normal should suspicion ever fall on him.

As each day went by and the body was not discovered Stillwell became more and more nervous. He visited the scene to confirm the girl was still there. That it had not been a bad dream. That the body had not been disturbed. But as each day passed there were horrible signs of insect and rodent interference. The smell was overwhelming and made him want to vomit. He did not feel remorse for the girl. Only for himself. Cross that he had allowed himself to get so carried away. On the one hand he felt in control. Only he knew how the girl had died and only he knew she *had* died. On the other hand, he wanted the body to be found and whatever was to happen next to happen. So he could get on his with his life one way or the other. If they linked the death to him then he'd have to tell them how it happened. How it was an accident. If they didn't then he'd got away with it, but he had learned his lesson. He'd not allow himself to get carried away like that again. Who knows, they might never find the body. By the end of summer the animals may have eaten the corpse to such an extent that she could never be identified.

Panic set in when he was in the Black Rabbit and he realised he was missing a dart. Straight away he thought it could have dropped out when he was visiting the body. He had not had it since the day in the park. He knew that. He had bent down over the body and had searched around the surrounding area for clues, clues that may have given him away. He had also lain down and masturbated near the body. He was sure that the dart had fallen out then. Rushing back to the body again, sweat broke out all over him as he searched with his hands everywhere, looking for the orange flight of the dart. It should be easy to find. Where was it? Where, for Christ's sake, was the fucking dart? He went back and looked again but became terrified that if the body were found and his dart was discovered nearby he would be implicated. He decided to 'find' the body. It suddenly seemed a good idea. Who would suspect him? And it would cover him should the dart be found at a later date.

In the supposition above I make mention of Stillwell masturbating at the murder scene. The fact that he volunteered to police in his statements about regularly masturbating and 'making water' when aroused in the park leads me to believe that there was a reason for his telling police this when there was no need to. He was concerned that traces of his semen would be found near the body, and should he be presented with such damning evidence this is how he intended to deal with such a development,

Stillwell knew that how he behaved on finding the body was crucial. He mustn't slip up. He convinced himself that he was going for a walk and that he stumbled on the dead girl. He feigned horror and panic and ran to the keeper's lodge and borrowed the bike to ride to the police station. He forgot his act to an extent when he stopped and chatted calmly to George Chamberlain of the Black Rabbit outside the post office before entering the police station, once again wide-eyed. He had seen his mother on the way back and told her the truth, or part-truth, and she, knowing her son, was swift to try to ensure he would not be implicated in any way. Stillwell played the part of the regular village lad who had been unlucky enough to find a dead body the best he could. Despite a few hiccups at some early police interviews it was a part he played successfully for the rest of his days.

25

AN EXTRAORDINARY COINCIDENCE

While researching the Arundel murder in 2010 a friend lent me a book called *A Rose Beyond the Thames*. It was written by Michael de Larrabeiti and published in 1978. My friend thought I would enjoy it, as the author recounts his childhood and adolescence in Battersea during the 1930s, 1940s and 1950s. I had written a semi-fictional account of my grandmother's hundred-year life named *Battersea Girl*, and there were obvious parallels.

My friend was correct, as I thoroughly enjoyed the book and immediately wanted to find out some more about the author. Sadly, Michael de Larrabeiti had died in 2008, but he left a legacy of work, and I ordered some of his other titles. One was called *Foxes' Oven*, a novel written in 2002, and although something made me pick this one out it was not until I opened it and started reading that I understood I had to put the book down, take a deep breath and reassure myself that I was not the victim of some elaborate hoax. I was not, but the stunning coincidence I will detail ranks among the stranger things that have happened to me in my life.

The cover of the book features an illustration of a cottage in a valley at the bottom of a slope with a snake of smoke puffing out the chimney. The cover blurb reads as follows:

> The year is 1940 and Becky Taylor, a young evacuee from London, arrives at Foxes' Oven, a gloomy house in the hamlet of Offham, some two miles from the town of Arundel. There she begins a new life with Agnes Clemmer and her family.
>
> During the summer months Becky discovers happiness, a sense of belonging and even love. But there are secrets in Foxes' Oven and Becky also discovers, at first hand, passion, jealousy, betrayal and violence. The horrific

events of those days are to haunt her for nearly half a century until, in her old age, hidden truths are revealed and Becky comes, at last, to confront the pains and ghosts of her childhood.

Foxes' Oven? Offham? Arundel? Of course, I recognised the name and the cover picture. Foxes' Oven was the Stillwell family home. The one that I had seen pictures of in the newspaper coverage of Thomas Stillwell's arrest. I opened the book and read on, dumbfounded and excited, until I finished it in one breathless, heart-pumping session.

It is the story of a girl evacuated during the Second World War from London to Arundel and placed with a family on the very rural outskirts of the town. Offham, to be exact. The dominant mother of the family is Agnes. *Thomas Stillwell's mother was Ethel Agnes.* She has a kind but ineffective husband. *The police described Thomas Rawlins Stillwell as sodden with drink and unreliable.* The husband had been a sailor. *Thomas Rawlins Stillwell lived on a naval pension.* His relationship with Agnes is strained because he believes that one of the sons is not his. *Thomas Stillwell senior harboured the same suspicions, according to the police.* The family house in the story is Foxes' Oven. *The Stillwell family house* was *Foxes' Oven* and de Larrabeiti is certainly describing the *same* house.

The local pub in the book, as in life, is the Black Rabbit. Agnes' oldest son is called Frank, and as the story unfolds it is revealed he is the murderer of a young woman from London. Despite his crime Agnes fiercely defends him and protects him from detection. *She washes some clothes and burns others. Frank has strange sexual habits, including voyeurism, and is said to enjoy lying under trains as they rattle over to him to gain thrills.* His younger brother is decent and kind. *Police described one of Tom's brothers in the same vein.*

It is an atmospheric and gripping read with a final twist that has a personal resonance for me, as the heroine of the book, Becky Taylor, spends her adult years living in a psychiatric hospital. The hospital named is Springfield in South London. My father was a senior administrator there for many years, including at the time the fictional Becky Taylor was there. If fact and fiction had merged they would have known one another.

Fact and fiction must have been merged in *Foxes' Oven*. Michael de Larrabeiti was evacuated to Arundel in 1940, eight years before Joan Woodhouse was murdered. Did he stay at Foxes' Oven with the Stillwells?

If he didn't he has certainly portrayed a very similar family dynamic and one that would not have been known to the public at large during the publicity surrounding the murder.

Had the case made him reflect back on his childhood experience of staying at that cottage with the then seventeen-year-old Stillwell perhaps? Did some personal knowledge of him convince the author that Stillwell was guilty of Joan's murder when the story broke in 1948? And towards the end of his life did Michael de Larrabeiti write *Foxes' Oven* to address the injustice and tragedy he felt had been visited on Joan Woodhouse and her family? Setting the story in the real house of the murder suspect was a bold literary move and could have resulted in some awkward questions.

Perhaps Michael de Larrabeiti's children or those close to him know the answers. He may have confided in them. How many more clues did he leave in that book, clues I have not picked up?

As the years roll by there are fewer and fewer people alive who *know* who killed Joan Woodhouse. There will be some. Some people in Arundel, though, think they know, still. In the summer of 2010 I visited with my daughter. We walked past Swanbourne Lake and up to Box Copse. I looked for the carving in the tree made by Joan's aunts, but to no avail. Its seclusion from the main path remains chilling.

We took tea in the lodge by the gates and overlooking the lake. I struck up a conversation with a helper. Did she remember the murder?

'How old do you think I am?' she said feigning offence. 'Not really, I was only about five. But I knew all about it. We all knew the man who did it. At least, we knew the man it was said did it. He was found not guilty, wasn't he?'

'It never got to trial by jury, actually.'

'Oh well, you know more than me. I do know something, though. This park is haunted. I wouldn't come in here at night. That's for certain. A lot of people have seen ghosts in here . . .'

Michelle and I looked at one another, wondering if we were stepping on to the set of a Hammer Horror film.

Later, in the pub near the 'new' police station, I managed to engage some locals about the murder. The barman named the accused man and said 'everyone' knew he did it, but he had led a blameless life afterwards, as if, in his eyes, that made it acceptable.

An old man was asked about it. He was gruff.

'What do you reckon, George?' asked the barman of the man. 'You knew the man we are talking about. Did he do it?'

The old man seemed reluctant to answer, and for a few seconds looked into his glass as if the answer was floating at the bottom. Eventually he replied, 'Well, if he didn't do it then I expect Glenn Miller will walk in that door any second now.'

Thomas Stillwell died in 2008, having outlived most of the people who figure in this book. He lost his father in 1955, his mother in 1976 and his brother Arthur in 2005. Thomas's wife passed away in 2014. She and Tom are buried in separate plots in separate cemeteries.

Fred Narborough enjoyed a TV career, appearing as 'the custodian of questions' on the extremely popular *The 64,000 Question* on ITV, as well as other various TV appearances.

Unfortunately for him he failed to declare the earnings from this show to the Inland Revenue, and he was pursued and forced to settle.

Later he became a security adviser to Rupert Murdoch following his launch of the *Sun* in London in the 1960s. He was fortunate not to have been connected to another potentially disastrous headline case. In 1970 two brothers named Arthur and Nizamodeen Hosein had watched Rupert Murdoch being interviewed on David Frost's TV show and decided it would be a good idea to kidnap Murdoch's wife and demand a ransom. They went to Bouverie Street and mistook Alick McKay, one of Murdoch's executives, for Murdoch as he was getting into a Rolls-Royce. They followed him back to Wimbledon then went back later and kidnapped his wife. Muriel McKay's body was never found, but the brothers were eventually convicted of murder. Poor Mrs McKay, it is widely believed, was fed to the pigs by the kidnappers.

Fred Narborough died in 1992 in his ninetieth year after enjoying a long and active retirement. In 2013 I located his daughter Jeanne, the same lady who must have been embarrassed when her father complained to her employer that she was earning too much money.

She remembered the Joan Woodhouse case all too well. She confirmed it had disturbed her father in many ways. She remembers he was distressed early in the investigation because Joan was wearing the same type of sandals that she herself wore. She said he had nightmares about the case and that he would wake during the night in cold sweats. He was 100 per cent convinced that Thomas Stillwell murdered Joan Woodhouse, she is sure, and it was to his eternal regret that a conviction was not secured. She was glad that he did manage to enjoy a long retirement and immersed himself in golf. She spoke of him with great affection and pride.

Prosecution lawyer Stuart Bass passed away in 1982, and Thomas Jacks, the tenacious private detective, lived until 1970. John Woodhouse died in the same year, outlived by his sisters-in-law Ida and Annie, who died in 1981 and 1988, respectively. Hartley Shawcross became Lord Shawcross and enjoyed the longest lifespan of them all, attaining his century before his passing in 2003.

In 2011 I was given permission by Sussex Police to review their files on the case. They were extremely helpful and informed me that they had reviewed the case themselves in 2010 as part of their initiative to re-examine unresolved cases. I do not know the outcome of that inquiry, but as nothing has transpired one can only assume they found no new evidence or anything on which they felt they could reopen the case. One would have hoped some evidence had been preserved and that DNA tests could have provided some resolution.

The files are expansive. I learned from them that Inspector Spooner makes no reference to his suspicion of suicide in his lengthy report. I read Inspector Narborough's theory as to who did it and the motive:

> Stillwell was utterly conceited. I submit that the rebuff he received from Joan Woodhouse may well have been the cause of her death. That she was savagely attacked there is no doubt.

But, more than anything, the most telling line in all the files is in a memorandum from Justice Travers Humphreys. It reveals his private reasoning as to why he rejected the private indictment – why he effectively killed the family's long and tortuous quest for justice. It is there, clearly written:

> I am 99% sure of Stillwell's guilt. But the fact of the matter remains that he was not cautioned at interview and therefore the key evidence of his statements will be ruled as inadmissible if we proceed to court.

This, then, is the heart of the matter. Stillwell was not charged and tried, not because there was not sufficient evidence or there was serious doubt over his guilt. He was allowed to go free, and several more lives were allowed to be blighted, to spare the feelings and reputation of a police officer who made the most basic errors in conducting this investigation and to maintain the credibility of Scotland Yard. It is there, buried in a file, in black and white in West Sussex Record Office.

EPILOGUE

During the course of writing this book I appealed on various Arundel and Sussex websites for any information surrounding the case. I received a variety of letters and emails. Many were anonymous, and the information and gossip contained therein I treated with caution. However, one local rumour, or myth, surfaced from three different sources. They came from people claiming to be older residents of Arundel or the children or grandchildren of older residents.

In the years after the murder the whisper in Arundel from some was that Thomas Stillwell was the illegitimate son of the 16th Duke of Norfolk, the much-loved Duke Bernard. The story goes that he had enjoyed a liaison with Tom's mother Ellen Agnes when he was a young lad of fifteen or sixteen. Ellen was seven years older, and we know that at some point she had worked in Arundel Castle, potentially taking her into the orbit of the young future duke. The rumour continues that the duke, while never admitting responsibility, arranged for Ellen to have the use of the Foxes' Oven cottage on the estate. The duke also, according to this story, covered Tom's legal fees when he was accused of Joan Woodhouse's murder.

It's the sort of story that one might expect to hear in a small town that has an unsolved murder hanging over it. The age difference made me sceptical, although after speaking to some academics and historians I became less circumspect. The practice of aristocrats impregnating servants is as old as the hills, it seems, and for a sixteen-year-old soon-to-be-duke raging with hormones to take advantage of a deferential servant girl older than him is not beyond the realms of possibility. Still, I would have paid it little credence and did just that until I saw by chance a photographic portrait of Duke Bernard. The likeness with Thomas Stillwell is uncanny. As he looks out at you the eyes, nose and mouth could be Stillwell's. There is no doubt there is a strong facial resemblance. It may be because of this that the rumour gained momentum in the first instance.

Then I recalled the remarks I had seen in the police files about Thomas Rawlins Stillwell. The police said he was an unreliable witness because he resented the boy and strongly believed he was not his biological father. Yet he had married Ellen shortly before Tom's birth in 1924. With a quarter-of-a-century age difference, it was an uncommon coupling.

My curiosity about the theory piqued, I reread Michael de Larrabeiti's *Foxes' Oven*. I saw the book in a whole new light. Remember the book is set in 1940 in a real house in a real town – Foxes' Oven in Offham. The family consists of a matriarch called Agnes (the real-life Ellen's middle name); there are two sons – one is decent, one is a sexually violent. One goes to war; one does not. Ellen's husband Harry is a drunk, a former merchant seaman who does not believe that one son is genetically his own. A land girl from London is murdered. There is a character called Joan. The book positively drips with hints and clues to those who have knowledge of the 1948 murder. My rereading confirmed to me that the author not only wanted to make life uncomfortable for the then still living Thomas Stillwell (without triggering a lawsuit), but he also knew plenty that was not in the public domain. In addition it is clear that Michael de Larrabeiti was, at the very least, aware of the Duke Bernard rumours. The following are extracts from the book:

'My mum says Agnes was in service for a year or two when she left school, at the castle.' Lucy wagged a finger at me as if she had heard all the gossip ever recounted. 'Blue blood in Billy,' my mum says, 'you can't mistake blue blood, it shines through the skin.'

Harry pushed his chair back. 'You weren't short of money.' He began shouting. 'You got it from someone . . . plenty of it.'

Billy lowered his eyes. 'We don't look like each other, Ma. Frank and me . . . people always say it.'

'You know what they talk about as soon as Offham is mentioned, or Foxes' Oven?'

'About Billy?'

'Yes, his father is the duke.'

This only proves that Michael de Larrabeiti had heard the stories, or possibly even that he started them. (Although the rumour seems to have been well established long, long before *Foxes' Oven* was released.) However, the physical likeness between the two men, especially when younger, is arresting. The fact that Ellen worked in the castle as a servant and therefore most likely came into regular contact with the duke is intriguing. Even more tantalising, however, is that on checking the Land Registry I discovered that the Duke of Norfolk did indeed sell Foxes' Oven to Ellen Agnes Stillwell in 1951, the year after it was found there was no case to answer for her son. No price, if there were any, is mentioned.

Where would a working countrywoman with a lazy, 'drink-sodden' husband have found the resources to purchase the cottage from the duke, given that family coffers would have recently been stretched or exhausted by paying her son's legal fees? Why would Duke Bernard have sold the cottage anyway? In more recent times the cottage was back in the estate's possession again, indicating that somewhere along the line it was repurchased. Why is the cottage sold just to Ellen and not Ellen and her husband?

A scenario can be imagined. Ellen, a sexually experienced young servant girl, catches the eye of the boy aristocrat, his young hormones raging. A romantic encounter occurs, the older woman flattered by her master's attention or feeling too deferential to reject his approaches. Ellen falls pregnant, but being in a relationship with a man twenty-five years her senior, whose pension, she hopes, will provide some measure of financial security for her and her two existing children, passes the child off as his. However, she has told Duke Bernard but has reassured him that she will not rock any boats. She knows the family depends on him for their work and shelter.

For a quarter of a century she keeps her word. Then the worst calamity befalls her special son. The one she knows has blue blood in him. He is suspected and then accused of murder. She knows it looks bad for him. She knows he could hang. She is desperate. And desperate times call for desperate measures.

Ellen seeks an audience with the duke, now a very powerful and influential grown man. The duke agrees. Bernard displays some scepticism that Thomas is actually his. He changes his mind when Ellen produces some photographs from her handbag. The thought of even a former servant claiming (not proving) that she has given birth to an illegitimate son who looks just like him terrifies him. The scenario of that alleged bastard son being tried, convicted and hanged for murder was a notion he could not even contemplate. There were potential implications, for him, Arundel, the dukedom, the aristocracy and, by association, even the royal family.

Duke Bernard says he will look after Tom's legal costs. Leave it to him. He resolves to do what he can to divert the tentacles of justice away from Tom – and, indirectly, himself. How or if he did that, Ellen would never know. Some people thought they knew. Some people – locals – who had their suspicions as to Tom's parentage thought they knew why, despite everything pointing to Stillwell, he never faced a jury.

Once the case against Tom did not materialise Tom and Ellen were not the only people to breathe a huge sigh of relief. The duke felt some gratitude towards Ellen for not panicking in her hour of need and engineering to some extent the 'right' outcome. He gifted her the cottage, hoping she would never be forced to seek his help again.

Earlier in this book I posed the following question: '*Why then, when there was far more reason for the police to believe that Stillwell was guilty than there was years later in the case of Stagg, did they not pursue him in the same way they did his 1990s equivalent? It cannot have been in the apparent weaknesses in the case against him but must have been rooted in the investigation itself. What other possible reason could there have been? There was no threat to national security. No notable people to protect.*'

Were this rumour to be true then perhaps there *were* issues of national security at stake and notable people to protect. Stranger things have happened.

Best stop here, as I am stepping quite firmly into the realms of fiction. Fiction, like Michael de Labbareiti's book *Foxes' Oven*.

TIMELINE

1921 Joan Mary Woodhouse is born in Barnsley to John and Nellie Woodhouse

1923 Thomas Rawlins Stillwell and Ellen Agnes Parson marry

1924 Thomas Philip George Stillwell is born in Arundel to Thomas Rawlins Stillwell and Ellen Agnes Stillwell

1940 Inspector Fred Narborough and future Attorney General Hartley Shawcross work together on interrogating wartime 'aliens'

1940 Author Michael de Larrabeiti is evacuated to Arundel

1943 Nellie Woodhouse dies of cancer

1946 Joan commits to her religious Rule of Life

1947 John Woodhouse remarries

1948 *Sunday 28 March* Joan makes a half-hearted suicide attempt

Tuesday 13 July Joan attends a party in north London

Saturday 17 July Joan celebrates her twenty-seventh birthday

Wednesday 28 July Joan mails letter to aunts indicating depressive state

Saturday 31 July

8 a.m. Joan takes breakfast at the YWCA in Greenwich

8.30 a.m. Joan leaves the hostel for 'home'

1 p.m. Joan's suitcase is deposited at Worthing Station

2 p.m. Trader sells bottle of Lembar to a girl he believes to be Joan (a bottle of Lembar is found by the body)

2.15 p.m. Witness believes she saw Joan Woodhouse walking towards Arundel Park

3 p.m. Thomas Stillwell says he was in Arundel Park between 2 p.m. and 4 p.m.

Thursday 5 August Telegram arrives at hostel from John Woodhouse wondering where Joan is

Hostel warden reports Joan missing to police

Saturday 7 August John Woodhouse and Aunt Ida arrive at hostel

Tuesday 10 August

4 p.m. Thomas Stillwell discovers body in Arundel Park

4.30 p.m. Stillwell meets publican George Chamberlain on way to police station

5 p.m. Thomas Stillwell arrives at police station to report finding body

Wednesday 11 August Inspector Narborough arrives in Arundel

Thursday 12 August Body identified in press as Joan Woodhouse

Friday 13 August Nicole Ashby gives evidence at the inquest in Arundel; inquest adjourned

Thursday 19 August Thomas Stillwell is called in to give a statement by Detective Inspector Dean

Monday 23 August Inspector Narborough interviews Thomas Stillwell for the first time

Tuesday 7 September Thomas Stillwell interviewed by police

Monday 27 September Narborough calls conference with Sussex police officers to brainstorm

Wednesday 29 September Aunt Ida meets Inspector Narborough and describes Joan's fondness for sunbathing

Saturday 9 October Detective Inspector Dean again interviews Thomas Stillwell

Tuesday 19 October Inspector Narborough has eight-hour interview with Thomas Stillwell

Wednesday 20 October Inspector Narborough has eleven-hour interview with Thomas Stillwell

Monday 22 November Resumed inquest opens and closes, concluding Joan was murdered by persons or persons unknown

1949 *Friday 7 January* Joan's aunts get audience with Inspector Narborough over dissatisfaction

Monday 10 October Thomas Jacks, a private detective hired by the Woodhouse family, arrives in Arundel

Tuesday 11 October Jacks meets Sergeant Bristow at Arundel Police Station

December Thomas Jacks submits his report to family and Scotland Yard, convinced he has compiled enough evidence to justify charging Stillwell

1950 *Sunday 19 February* Scotland Yard reopens case; Inspector Spooner is dispatched to Arundel

Sunday 26 February Stillwell sells story to *Sunday Pictorial*

Wednesday 1 March The *Yorkshire Post* reveals that there is a little hope of an arrest, despite Spooner not having completed his investigations

April Inspector Spooner completes probe

May Inspector Spooner submits report to DPP and concludes no further action can be justified

Friday 4 August Thomas Jacks and John Woodhouse apply for a private prosecution for murder

Wednesday 9 August Inspector Spooner travels to Bridlington to brief the Woodhouse family and Lena Bamber

Wednesday 30 August

5.50 p.m. Warrant issued for Stillwell's arrest

6.15 p.m. Detective Inspector Dean arrests Thomas Stillwell at Foxes' Oven for murder

Thursday 31 August Thomas Stillwell is refused bail at Littlehampton and is taken to Brixton Prison

Thursday 14 September Mrs Petley picks out Thomas Stillwell in an ID parade; her friend does not

Tuesday 19 September Committal hearing in Arundel begins

Wednesday 20 September Mrs Stillwell gives evidence at committal hearing

Thursday 21 September End of the Crown's case

Friday 22 September Magistrates decide no case for Thomas Stillwell to answer; Stillwell attends celebration dinner at Chichester hotel

Saturday 23 September Stillwell pictured shopping in Guildford

Sunday 24 September Newspapers carry accounts by Thomas Stillwell of his ordeal

Saturday 7 October Thomas Stillwell marries his fiancée

Monday 23 October Hartley Shawcross says in Parliament that the Arundel case was handled justly

Friday 1 December Mr Justice Humphreys refuses a bill for indictment in the case of Stillwell

1955 Thomas Rawlins Stillwell dies

1963 Reg Spooner dies

1970 Thomas Jacks dies

John Woodhouse dies

1976 Ellen Agnes Stillwell dies

1992 Fred Narborough dies

2002 *Foxes' Oven* by Michael de Larrabeiti is published

2003 Hartley Shawcross dies

2008 Thomas Stillwell dies

POSTSCRIPT

In 2013 I applied to have sight of the files held at the National Archive on the case under the Freedom of Information Act. They released some papers to me, which mainly consisted of correspondence between the legal entities involved and threw very little new light on the case. However, they refused to open other files, which contained letters from the public among other things. Also, they said, information on the suspect that could compromise his privacy, were he alive, was contained therein. These files will remain closed until 2025 and 2033, seventy-seven and eighty-five years respectively from the date of the murder. Despite informing the National Archive that the suspect was dead, they refused my appeal. I firmly believe the answers to most of the questions raised in this book are in those files.

At the start of this book I refer to the photograph album dedicated to Joan and compiled lovingly by her aunts. As I packed the album up with other material for safe return to the Woodhouse family and Lena Bamber, guardian of Joan's memory, I found a note that I had somehow missed in my haste to work through it originally. It is written by either Ida or Annie. The final words of this book will be left to them:

Our beloved,
You were so lovely and beautiful in your life, so brave; so unassuming in purpose; so true to your ideals; so full of humour and wisdom but yet so childlike in your utter simplicity and joy in things lovely and of good report, so tender in your love and understanding.

We could not convey to others even the shadow of what you were. And when you left us you took with you the better part of us.

FURTHER READING

Adamson, Iain, *The Great Detective: A Life Of Deputy Commander Reginald Spooner Of Scotland Yard*, London: Frederick Muller, 1966

Cathcart, Brian, *The Case Of Stephen Lawrence*, London: Viking, 1999

De Larrabeiti, Michael, *Foxes' Oven*, London: Tallis House, 2008

Knight, Martin, *We Are Not Manslaughterers: The Murder Of Station Sergeant Thomas Green*, Newcastle upon Tyne: Tonto Books, 2010

Kynaston, David, *Austerity Britain 1945–1951*, London: Bloomsbury, 2008

Narborough, Fred, *Murder On My Mind*, London: Allan Wingate, 1959

Robey, Edward, *The Jester And The Court: Reminiscences*, London: William Kimber, 1976

Simpson, Professor Keith, *Forty Years Of Murder*, London: George G. Harrap and Company, 1978

INDEX OF NAMES

LONDON BOOKS

FLYING THE FLAG FOR
FREE-THINKING LITERATURE

www.london-books.co.uk

PLEASE VISIT OUR WEBSITE FOR

- Current and forthcoming books
  - Author and title profiles
    - Events and news
  - Secure on-line bookshop
- Recommendations and links
- An alternative view of London literature

London Classics

The Angel And The Cuckoo *Gerald Kersh*
Doctor Of The Lost *Simon Blumenfeld*
The Gilt Kid *James Curtis*
It Always Rains On Sunday *Arthur La Bern*
Jew Boy *Simon Blumenfeld*
May Day *John Sommerfield*
Night And The City *Gerald Kersh*
A Start In Life *Alan Sillitoe*
There Ain't No Justice *James Curtis*
They Drive By Night *James Curtis*
Wide Boys Never Work *Robert Westerby*